Frédéric Chopin

COMPOSER RESOURCE MANUALS
VOLUME 50
GARLAND REFERENCE LIBRARY OF THE HUMANITIES
VOLUME 1961

FRÉDÉRIC CHOPIN
A GUIDE TO RESEARCH

WILLIAM SMIALEK

GARLAND PUBLISHING, INC.
A MEMBER OF THE TAYLOR & FRANCIS GROUP
NEW YORK & LONDON
2000

Published in 2000 by
Garland Publishing, Inc.
A Member of the Taylor & Francis Group
19 Union Square West
New York, NY 10003

10   9   8   7   6   5   4   3   2   1

Library of Congress Cataloging-in-Publication Data
Smialek, William.
    Frédéric Chopin : a guide to research / William Smialek.
      p. cm. — (Composer resource manuals : v. 50) (Garland
reference library of the humanities : v. 1961)
    Discography: p.
    Includes index.
    ISBN 0-8153-2180-5 (alk. paper)
    1. Chopin, Frédéric, 1810–1849—Bibliography.   I. Title.
II. Series: Garland composer resource manuals : v. 50. III. Series:
Garland reference library of the humanities : vol. 1961.
ML134.C54S65   1999
016.7862'092—dc21   99-42566
                                            CIP

Printed on acid-free, 250-year-life paper.
Manufactured in the United States of America

Composer Resource Manuals

In response to the growing need for bibliographic guidance to the vast literature on significant composers, Garland is publishing an extensive series of research guides. This ongoing series encompasses more than 50 composers; they represent Western musical tradition from the Renaissance to the present century.

Each research guide offers a selective, annotated list of writings, in all European languages, about one or more composers. There are also lists of works by the composers, unless these are available elsewhere. Biographical sketches and guides to library resources, organizations, and specialists are presented. As appropriate to the individual composer, there are maps, photographs, or other illustrative matter, glossaries, and indexes.

To the memory of my father

Contents

Preface

Our understanding of Frédéric Chopin as a man and musician is marked with ambiguities. There are contradictions between his public and private styles, and his tranformations of popular genres. The known events of his life and relationships have long stimulated the imaginations of writers. Unusual tonal and structural elements of the music have given scholars much to ponder while they sort through the revisions that Chopin made to musical texts through creative and publishing processes. As a result of the quest to come to terms with the composer and his music, an immense body of literature has been published on Frédéric Chopin since his lifetime. Fortunately, bibliographies compiled by earlier scholars have classified the many books and articles about the composer and his music. Supplements to these Chopin bibliographies continue to offer excellent guidance for contemporary scholars. Nevertheless, these research tools do not include annotations nor other assessments of the content and value of this literature.

Frédéric Chopin: A Guide to Research is not intended as an exhaustive review of the immense body of literature on the composer, but as a resource identifying key directions in Chopin scholarship for scholars and other musicians new to Chopin studies. I have reviewed selected references in European and Slavic languages (English, German, French, Polish, and to a lesser extent Italian, Russian, and Czech) which are likely to provide assistance and information. The research guide concentrates on post–World War II scholarship and attempts to isolate trends in recent research. Some of the references are easily consulted in most prominent music libraries, whereas other specialized publications, although of value to researchers, may be more difficult to access. The research guide was generated from a collection of over 1,500 bibliographic citations, books, and articles on Chopin, his milieux, and related cultural information. The primary sources of these references include *RILM, Music Index,* and the Michałowski bibliographies. I have given particular attention to collections of research articles on Chopin, most notably *Rocznik Chopinowski* and the various publications with the title *Chopin Studies.* Given the frequency that Chopin's piano works are performed, there are many dissertations on Chopin's music. As performance-oriented studies predominate, I have not included any dissertations among the selected resources in this volume.

Chopin's life has been examined from a variety of perspectives. To assist in the coordination of life events, I have constructed a chronology that lists the main events in the composer's life. The publication of many of his works is noted by date; an exact date of composition is more elusive. The list of published biographies of Chopin reaches back well into the nineteenth century. The number of reprint editions attests to the importance of the composer. Although several of these volumes could be designated as those most important, the longer list transmits subtle developments in myths that have generated about Chopin.

Chopin's name is used in the common French version, unless a source title cites it otherwise. Other Polish names appear in that language, except when another version of the name is given on the title page of the reference. Alternate versions of an author's name are possible in the case of translations or books published in different countries—for example, Casimir Wierzynski and Kazimierz Wierzyński. Polish place names are given as they appear in the actual reference; some Polish publications were intended for a foreign market and carry English versions of the publications information. I do use the English version of the Polish capital, Warsaw, especially in the chronology of Chopin's life and catalog of letters. Titles of Chopin's compositions, the most common referring to a genre, appear in English. The original forms of titles are given in the index.

The literature makes clear that the primary source of information about Chopin is his vast correspondence, augmented with letters by other cultural figures that mention or comment on the composer's activities. Beyond listing the prominent collections of Chopin letters, the *Guide to Research* provides an extensive catalog to the published letters. Annotation of the individual letters is beyond the scope of this book, and in any case, editions of the correspondence are readily found in libraries.

The intention of the catalog is to assist researchers in locating specific letters in order to compare texts, translations, dates, and transcriptions from the originals.

Several publications list sound recordings of Chopin's music through the LP era. The discography included in this volume in intended to update these discographies with recordings available on compact disc. Prominent Chopin performers were selected from listings in the *Schwann Opus* and *Gramophone Classical* catalogs. An effort has been made to provide recordings of all the works. Consequently, the listing of the best Chopin works are limited and subjectively chosen.

In compiling this *Guide to Research*, I have relied on several music collections to provide access to the materials. The effort to review each resource cited was concentrated in the music libraries of the University of Illinois, the University of North Texas, and Harvard University. My thanks to the staff members of each institution for their assistance. I have also freely sought out information on-line in the catalogs of the Library of Congress and other institutions. I owe special gratitude to the members of my family—Molly, Andrew, and Adam—for their support throughout this project.

William Smialek
Midway College

FRÉDÉRIC CHOPIN

CHAPTER 1

Biography: A Chronology of Events in Chopin's Life

1810   *1 March*: Born at Żelazowa Wola, near Warsaw (baptismal certificate indicates date of birth as 22 February 1810); son of Justyna Krzyżanowska (1782–1861) and Nicolas Chopin (1771–1844). Family moves to Warsaw. Siblings: Ludwika [Jędrzejewicz] (1807–1855), Izabella [Barczińska](1811–1881), Emilia (1812–1827).

1816   Studies with Wojciech Żywny beginning at age 6.

1817   Composes Polonaise in G minor, dedicated to Countess Skarbek, published by J.J. Cybulski in 1830.

1818   Publicly performs piano concerto of Adalbert Gyrowetz at age of 8. Performs in aristocratic salons, 1818–1819.

1820   *January:* Presented to Italian soprano Angelica Catalani. Dedicates *Military March* to Russian Grand Duke Constantine.

1822   Begins studies with Józef Elsner.

1823   *24 February:* Performs concerto of Ferdinand Ries. Enters Warsaw Lyceum.

1824   Vacations in Szafarnia. "Publishes" *Szarfarnia Courier* with sister. Performs concerto of Frédéric Kalkbrenner. *September:* Enters fifth form of Lyceum.

1825   Rondo for Piano, op. 1, published in Warsaw. *10 June:* Performs on aeolomelodikon. *7 July:* Performs for Czar Alexander I. *Summer:* Vacations in Szafarnia.

1826   *February:* First comments about poor health. *August–September:* Visits spa at Duszniki. *Fall:* Attends Szkoło Główno Muzyki.

1827   Elsner's notes on Chopin's examination—"szczególna zdolność" [especially talented].

1828   *Rondo à la Mazur*, op. 5, published in Warsaw. *September:* Travels to Berlin. *October:* Two days in Poznań.

1829   *April–October:* Infatuation with Konstancja Gladowska (1810–1880). *July:* Completes studies at Szkoło Główno Muzyki. *Summer:* Travels to Vienna. *11 August:* Concert in Vienna at the Kärntnerthortheater. *18 August:* Concert in Vienna at the Kärntnerthortheater. *19 August:* Travels to Prague and Dresden. *[August]:* Arranges to have Variations on "La ci darem la mano" published by Haslinger as op. 2. *20 October:* Visits Wiesalowski and Razdziwiłł estates.

1830   *17 March:* Public performance of Piano Concerto in F minor, op. 21, and Fantasy in A major at Teatr Narodowy, orchestra directed by Karol Kurpiński. *8 July:* Performs Variations, op. 2, in concert at Teatr Narodowy. *11 October:* Performs Piano Concerto in E minor, op. 11, at Teatr Narodowy. *1 November:* Leaves Warsaw. *6 November:* Wrocław. *10 November:* Dresden. *23 November:* Arrives in Vienna. *28 November:* Beginning of insurrection in Warsaw. *Winter, 1830–1831:* Vienna.

1831   Publishes Introduction and Polonaise for Violoncello, op. 3. *11 June:* Performs Concerto in E minor in concert. *28 August:* Concert in Munich. *September:* Arrives in Paris after journey through Linz, Salzburg, Munich, and Stuttgart (Stuttgart Diary). Resides in Paris at Boulevard Poissonnière 27. *8 September:* Russians occupy Warsaw. *21 September:* Piano Concerto in E minor, op. 11, recognized in *Allgemeine musikalische Zeitung*. *17 November:* Meets Delfina Potocka. *7 December:* Schumann recognizes Chopin in *Allgemeine musikalische Zeitung*.

1832   Publishes Mazurkas, opp. 6 and 7; Trio for Violoncello and Piano, op. 8; and Nocturnes, op. 9. Develops friendships with Mendelssohn and Berlioz. *26 February:* First Paris concert. *March/April:* Turns to teaching. *20 May:* Concert at great hall of the Conservatoire sponsored by Princess de la Moskova. *June–July:* Moves to Rue Cité Benère 4. *December:* Beginning of friendship with August Franchomme.

1833   Becomes friends with Vincenzo Bellini. Publishes Études, op. 10; Concerto in E minor, op. 11; Variations, op. 12; and Nocturnes, op. 15. *2 April:* Performance with Franz Liszt. *3 April:* Performance with Liszt. *June:* Address change to Chaussée d'Antin 5. *15 December:* Chopin performs with Liszt at Conservatoire concert.

1834   Publishes Fantasia in A major, op. 13; Rondo à la Krakowiak, op. 14; Rondo in E-flat major, op. 16; Grand duo concertante; Mazurkas, op. 17; Waltz, op. 18; and Bolero, op. 19. *May:* Travels to Germany with Ferdinand Hiller; met Felix Mendelssohn, Clara and Robert Schumann. *7 December:* Appears on Berlin concert. *14 December:* Takes part in concert with Hector Berlioz. *25 December:* Appears in concert with Liszt.

1835   Publishes Scherzo in B minor, op. 20. *25 February:* Plays two-piano duets with Hiller at the Erard salon. *22 March:* Concert at the Pleyel Hall. *4 April:* Polish benefit concert at the Théâtre Italien. *26 April:* Performs Andante spianato and grande polonaise in E-flat, op. 22, on last public performance. *29 May:* Meeting with Adam Mickiewicz. *1835, 1836:* Visits Germany. *15 August:* Meets family at Karlsbad; Dresden-Leipzig-Heidelberg-Paris. *September:* Meets Maria Wodzińska in Dresden.

1836   Publishes Concerto in F minor, op. 21; Andante spianato, op. 22; Ballade in G minor, op. 23; Mazurkas, op. 24; Polonaises, op. 26; and Nocturnes, op. 27. *9 April:* Liszt farewell concert at Erard salon. *July:* Meets with parents of Maria Wodzińska at Marienbad-Leipzig. *9 September:* Engagement to Maria Wodzińska; not sanctioned by her father and kept private. *11–13 September:* Meets with Schumann in Leipzig. Change of address to Rue Chaussée d'Antin 38. *October–November:* Meets George Sand.

1837 Publishes Études, op. 25; Impromptu, op. 29; Scherzo in B minor, op. 31; and Nocturnes, op. 32. *10 July:* Travels with Camille Pleyel to London for two weeks.

1838 Publishes Mazurkas, opp. 30 and 33, and Waltzes, op. 34. *2 March:* Concert appearance with Alkan, Gutmann, Zimmerman. *March:* Performs Piano Concerto in E minor, op. 11, at Rouen. *May:* Romance with Sand develops. *Winter 1838–1839:* Chopin accompanies Sand to Majorca. *1 November:* Meets Sand and her children at Perpignan. *7 November:* Boards ship for winter in Majorca.

1839 Publishes Preludes, op. 28. *25 February:* Arrives in Marseilles. *28 April:* Plays organ at A. Nourrit funeral. *22 May:* Travels from Marseilles to Nohant. *Summer:* At George Sand's estate in Nohant. *October:* Accepts Friederike Muller as student (she kept diary). *11 October:* Moves from Rue Tronchet 5 to share apartment at Rue Pigalle 16.

1840 Lives in Paris with George Sand. Publishes Sonata in B-flat minor, op. 35; Impromptu, op. 36; Nocturnes, op. 37; Ballade in F major, op. 38; Scherzo in C-sharp minor, op. 39; Polonaises, op. 40; Mazurkas, op. 41; and Waltz op. 42.

1841 Publishes Tarantella, op. 43; Polonaise, op. 44; Prelude in C-sharp minor, op. 45; Allegro de concert, op. 46; Ballade in A-flat major, op. 47; Nocturnes, op. 48; and Fantaisie, op. 49. *26 April:* Concert with soprano Laure Damoreau-Cinti at Salle Pleyel. *18 June–4 November:* Nohant

1842 Publishes Mazurkas, op. 50. *21 February:* Concert with Pauline Viardot-Garcia and August Franchomme at Salle Pleyel. *20 March:* Plays at Czartoryski's. *6 May–27 September:* Summer in Nohant. Returns to Paris to reside at Square d'Orléans 9 (George Sand at No. 5).

1843 Publishes Impromptu, op. 51; Ballade in F minor, op. 52; Polonaise, in A-flat major, op. 53; and Scherzo, op. 54. *22 May–28 October:* Summer in Nohant.

1844 Publishes Nocturnes, op. 55, and Mazurkas, op. 56. *3 May:* Father dies. *28 May–28 November:* Resident at Nohant. *13 August–*

3 September: Ludwika Jędrzejewicz (Chopin's sister) and husband visit.

1845   Publishes Berceuse, op. 57; Sonata in B minor, op. 58; and Mazurkas, op. 59. *13 June–28 November:* Nohant.

1846   Publishes Barcarolle, op. 60; Polonaise-fantaisie, op. 61; and Nocturnes, op. 62. *April:* Tours. *May–November:* Nohant. *25 June:* Serial publication of George Sand's *Lucrezia Floriani.* *29 June:* Quarrels with Maurice Sand. *November:* Leaves Nohant for last time.

1847   Publishes Mazurkas, op. 63; Waltzes, op. 64. Departs from George Sand. *20 May:* Solange Sand marries Jean-Baptiste-August Clésinger.

1848   Publishes Sonata in G minor for Violoncello and Piano, op. 65. *16 February:* Last concert in Paris. *20 April:* Arrives in London for tour of England and Scotland. *15 May:* Performs at Stafford House. *23 June:* Performs at Eaton Place. *7 July:* Performs at St. James Square with Pauline Viardot-Garcia. *5 August:* Calder House. *28 August:* Concert in Manchester. *27 September:* Concert in Glasgow. *4 October:* Concert in Edinburgh.

1849   *January:* Returns to Paris. *March:* Gift of 25,000 francs from Jane Stirling. *Summer:* In Chaillot. *8 August:* Ludwika arrives. *9 September:* 12 Place Vendôme. *30 September:* Consultation of physicians. *15 October:* Visited by Delfina Potocka. *17 October:* Dies in Paris about 2 a.m. *30 October:* Funeral at the Madeleine. Mozart *Requiem* performed. Burial at Père-Lachaise Cemetery, Paris.

CHAPTER 2

Reference Works

BIBLIOGRAPHIES

The literature on Chopin has been well documented over the decades of the twentieth century. The collected bibliographic citations vary a great deal, however, in their value to Chopin researchers. Kornel Michałowski represents the most consistent direction in Polish music bibliography. His many publications include listings of printed sources of information on Polish music in general, which are supplemented by bibliographic articles published in selected journals such as *Polish Music* and *Polish Musicological Studies*. More specialized are the bibliographic works specifically on Chopin. An annual compilation of sources on Chopin appears in *Rocznik Chopinowski* (1970–). The Michałowski bibliographies include references in newspapers and minor Polish publications. As thorough as the cataloging and classifying of sources is, the citations are not accompanied by annotations.

1.   Melville, Derek. *Chopin: A Biography, with a Survey of Books, Editions, and Recordings.* Hamden, Conn.: Linnet Books, 1977. 108 p.   ISBN 0208015426   ML 410.C54 M47

Review: Jill Foulkes, *Brio* 14, no. 1 (Spring 1977): 22–23.
     The biography, encompassing pages 7–61, is a summary of the available documentation. It reproduces short quotations from the Chopin letters. The bibliographic essay discusses the letters and biographies, as well as criticism and analyses of music. Contains a discography and index.

2.   Tomaszewski, Mieczysław. "Chopin." In *Encyklopedia Muzy-czna PWM, Część biograficzna*, ed. Elżbieta Dziębowska, C-D, 108–192. Kraków: Polskie Wydawnictwo Muzyczne, 1984. ISBN 8322402236 t. 2

A long encyclopedia article that addresses all aspects of Chopin research, including his life, musical style, genres of composition, aesthetics, performance history, reception, mythology, and influence. Many small reproductions support the text. Includes a chronology, list of works, and extensive bibliography.

3.   Michałowski, Kornel. *Bibliografia polskiego piśmiennictwa muzycznego* [Bibliography of Polish writing on music]. Materiały do bibliografii muzyki polskiej, 3. Kraków: Polskie Wydawnictwo Muzyczne, 1955. 280 p.   ML 120.P6 M5

Covers the period from the sixteenth century to 1954 and Polish dissertations from 1917 to 1954. Includes publications in Polish and works by Polish authors published in other languages. Categorizes 1,837 citations by subject matter, but the citations are not annotated. Includes author index.

4.   Michałowski, Kornel. *Bibliografia polskiego piśmiennictwa muzycznego. Suplement I* [Bibliography of Polish writing on music]. Materiały do bibliografii muzyki polskiej, 4. Kraków: Polskie Wydawnictwo Muzyczne, 1964. 203 p.   ML 120.P6 M5

5.   Michałowski, Kornel. *Bibliografia polskiego piśmiennictwa muzycznego. Suplement II* [Bibliography of Polish writing on music]. Materiały do bibliografii muzyki polskiej, 5. Kraków: Polskie Wydawnictwo Muzyczne, 1964. 464 p.   ML 120.P6 M5

6.   Michałowski, Kornel. *Bibliografia chopinowska 1849–1969*. Kraków: Polskie Wydawnictwo Muzyczne, 1970. 268 p.   ML 134.C54 M52

Lists 3,970 bibliographic citations classified into topics such as documents, life, works, interpretation, and reception. The bibliography is selective, but covering both the learned and popular literature. Emphasizes publications in Polish. Notes reviews of books. Includes subject and author indexes, as well as an index of Chopin works cited. The book is ornamented with reproductions of prominent publications.

Review: Adam Mrygoń, *Rocznik Chopinowski* 11 (1979): 173–176.

7. Michałowski, Kornel. "Bibliografia chopinowska 1970–1973." *Rocznik Chopinowski* 9 (1975): 121–178.

Includes reviews, newspaper articles, and minor publications in Polish. International in scope. Reveals multiple publication of some research.

8. Michałowski, Kornel. "Bibliografia chopinowska 1974–1977." *Rocznik Chopinowski* 11 (1978): 115–171.

9. Michałowski, Kornel. "Bibliografia chopinowska 1978." *Rocznik Chopinowski* 12 (1980): 225–234.

10. Michałowski, Kornel. "Bibliografia chopinowska 1979." *Rocznik Chopinowski* 13 (1981): 131–139.

11. Michałowski, Kornel. "Bibliografia chopinowska 1980." *Rocznik Chopinowski* 14 (1982): 61–76.

12. Michałowski, Kornel. "Bibliografia chopinowska 1981." *Rocznik Chopinowski* 15 (1983): 171–183.

13. Michałowski, Kornel. "Bibliografia chopinowska 1982." *Rocznik Chopinowski* 16 (1984): 153–162.

14. Michałowski, Kornel. "Bibliografia chopinowska 1983–1984." *Rocznik Chopinowski* 17 (1985): 215–233.

15. Michałowski, Kornel. "Bibliografia chopinowska 1985–1988." *Chopin Studies* 3 (1990): 319–363.

16. Michałowski, Kornel. "Bibliografia chopinowska 1985–1986." *Rocznik Chopinowski* 18 (1989): 201–240.

17. Michałowski, Kornel. "Bibliografia chopinowska 1987." *Rocznik Chopinowski* 19 (1987): 297–313.

18. Michałowski, Kornel. "Bibliografia chopinowska 1988–1989." *Rocznik Chopinowski* 20 (19): 264–289.

19. Michałowski, Kornel. "Bibliografia chopinowska 1991–1993." *Rocznik Chopinowski* 21 (1995): 276–336.

20.   Michałowski, Kornel. "Polish Dissertations in Musicology
       1947–1974." In *Polish Musicological Studies* 1, ed. Zofia
       Chechlińska and Jan Stęszewski, 261–269. Kraków: Polskie
       Wydawnictwo Muzyczne, 1977.   ML 5.P764

21.   Michałowski, Kornel. "Polish Dissertations in Musicology
       1973–1977." In *Polish Musicological Studies* 2, ed. Zofia
       Chechlińska and Jan Stęszewski, 341–344. Kraków: Polskie
       Wydawnictwo Muzyczne, 1985.   ISBN 8322402635   ML5.P764

       Lists several academic papers on Chopin. Information includes
English translations of titles.

22.   Michałowski, Kornel. "Refleksje chopinowskiego bibliografia."
       Rocznik Chopinowski 20 (1988): 93–99.

Each of the following catalogs of nineteenth-century periodicals is organized differently, but they all provide introductions on the periodicals
covered and are well indexed. Contemporary references to Chopin in the
Polish press can be researched with these aids.

23.   Michałowski, Kornel. *Gazeta Teatralna 1843–1844.* Biblio-
       grafia Polskich Czasopism Muzycznych 2. Kraków: Polskie
       Wydawnictwo Muzyczne, 1956. 75 p. AI15.M5

24.   Dziki, Sylwester. *Muzyka w polskich czasopismach literackich
       i społecznych 1831–1863.* Bibliografia Muzyczna Polskich Cza-
       sopism Niemuzycznych, 2. Kraków: Polskie Wydawnictwo
       Muzyczne, 1973. 169 p.   ML120.P6 B5 t.2

25.   Strumiłło, Dobrochna. *Tygodnik Muzyczny 1820–21; Pamiętnik
       Muzyczny Warszawski 1835–1836.* Bibliografia Polskich Cza-
       sopism Muzycznych, 1. Kraków: Polskie Wydawnictwo Muzy-
       czne, 1955. 114 p.   ML5.T945

26.   Sydow, Bronisław Edward. *Bibliografia F. F. Chopina.* War-
       szawa: Towarzystwa Naukowego Warszawskiego, 1949. 586 p.
       ML134.C54 S89

       Pioneering reference work published in honor of the Chopin year
1949. Bibliographical citations total 8,738 and include the author, title,
publication information, and date of each reference. A reference note is

provided if the title is obscure. The book is organized into sections such as works, biography, musicological studies, literary and musical works, reviews, and iconography. The references are international in scope, and cover nonmusical sources. The book includes a list of Chopin's works, index of names, subjects, and journals.

27.   Sydow, Bronisław Edward. *Bibliografia F. F. Chopina. Supplement.* Warszawa: Polskie Wydawnictwo Naukowe, 1954. 179 p. ML134.C54 S89

Continues the bibliography with citations 8,739 through 11,527. The indexes are consolidated into an alphabetical index and subject index.

28.   Smialek, William. *Polish Music: A Research and Information Guide.* New York: Garland, 1989. 260 p.   ISBN 082404615 ML120.P6S6 1989

A reference guide on all aspects of Polish music. The catagories of reference and research materials will guide scholars toward a more detailed search for information on Chopin and his contemporaries. The section on the nineteenth century covers materials in Polish and other European languages. Includes a discography and index.

29.   Turło, Teresa Dalila. "Bibliografia wydań dzieł Chopina 1969–1973." *Rocznik Chopinowski* 9 (1975): 177–178.

Lists publications of Chopin works, including transcriptions and anthologies. Contains six citations for the period 1969–1973.

Several bibliographic references are important for work with Polish publications. Although not solely devoted to music bibliography, they reference fine arts, historical research, and cultural history that may be of interest to the Chopin researcher.

30.   *Przewodnik bibliograficzny; Urzędowy wykaz druków wydanych w Polskiej Rzeczypospolitej Ludowej* [Bibliographic guide; official list of issued printed matter in the Polish People's Republic]. Warszawa: Biblioteka Narodowa, 1945–. ISSN 0033–2518 Z 2523.P93

A weekly publication of Polish publishing activity organized by subject categories. Category 78 is designated for books about music, with 78.089 reserved for printed music. Information provided includes ISBN, pagination, extra features outside of text, and the number of copies printed.

31.   Rondestevdt, Karen. "Organizing Chaos: Keeping Track of Current Publications Under the New Order in Poland." *Polish Review* 41, no. 2 (1996): 157–171.

Describes the bibliographic control of new publications under the socialist government. Explains problems that were created by the new economic conditions after 1989 and incentives for the many new book publishers to register their publications with the ISBN and ISSN offices. The information may be of use in tracking obscure Polish publications.

CATALOGS

A number of references are available to lead the researcher through the manuscripts of Chopin's works and collections of important archives.

32.   Kobylańska, Krystyna. *Rękopisy utworów Chopina: katalog* [Manuscripts of Chopin's works]. Kraków: Polskie Wydawnictwo Muzyczne, 1977. 2 vols.   ML 410.C54 D6 t.2

33.   Kobylańska, Krystyna. *Frederic Chopin: Thematisch-bibliographisches Werkverzeichnis.* München: G. Henle Verlag, 1979. 362 p. ISBN 3873280299   ML 134.C54 A315

Reviews: Jean-Jacques Eigeldinder, *Fontes artis musicae* 26, no. 2 (1979): 142–144; L. Michael Griffel, *Notes* 37, no. 4 (June 1981): 847–849; Jeffrey Kallberg, *Journal of the American Musicological Society* 34, no. 2 (1981): 357–365; Jeffrey Kallberg, *19th Century Music* 3, no. 2 (1979): 163–164; Zofia Lissa, *Muzyka* 23, no. 2 (1978): 85–88; *Ruch Muzyczny* 21, no. 19 (1977): 15–16.

Includes more information in the Polish version; for example, volume 2 reproduces plates of manuscripts that are not in the German version of the catalog. Polish edition does not include musical incipits. See Kallberg review in the *Journal of the American Musicological Society* for a detailed comparison of the Polish and German editions.

34. Brown, Maurice J.E. *Chopin: An Index of His Works in Chrono-logical Order*. 2nd ed. London: Macmillan, 1972. 214 p. ML 134.C54 B84 1972

Presents each Chopin work with its musical incipit, publication information, dedication, manuscript information, and other details about publication. The volume has extensive indices and appends lists of Chopin's addresses in Paris, the complete editions, autograph albums, publishers, and order of publishing.

35. Chominski, Józef Michał and Teresa Dalila Turło. *Katalog dziel Fryderyka Chopina* [A catalogue of the works of Frédéric Chopin]. Documenta chopiniana. Warszawa: Towarzystwo im. F. Chopina, 1990. 518 p. ISBN 8322404077 MI 134.C54 A18 1990

Lists extant autographs, copies, first editions, and subsequent prints, with reference to lost and doubtful works. Includes a summary in English and index.

36. Adamczyk-Schmid, Bożena. "Katalog zbiorów Muzeum Fry-deryka Chopina i George Sand w celi nr 2 Klasztoru Kartuzów w Valdemosie" [Catalog of the collection of the Frédéric Chopin and George Sand Museum in cell no. 2 of the Carthusian Cloister in Valldemosa]. *Rocznik Chopinowska* 18 (1989): 114–135.

A catalog of nine manuscripts. Contains full documentaion of each item with bibliographic notes.

37. Kobylańska, Krystyna. "Zbióry muzealne Towarzysta im. Fry-deryka Chopina w Warszawie" [The museum collection of the Chopin Society in Warsaw]. *Rocznik Chopinowska* 1 (1956): 304–323.

A catalog providing information on Chopin autographs, iconog-raphy, souvenirs, and letters. Additionally includes items related to Chopin's life and works.

38. Nectoux, Jean-Michel and Jean-Jacques Eigeldinger. "Edouard Ganche i jego kolekcja Chopinowska" [Edouard Ganche and his Chopin collection]. *Rocznik Chopinowski* 17 (1985): 235–251.

Catalogs 35 items, mostly manuscripts and iconography. A biog-raphy of Ganche is related by Nectoux; Eigeldinger discusses the musi-cological writings of the scholar.

39.   Himelfarb, Constance. "Le symposium musicologique interna-
        tional Chopin et le romantisme." *Revue de musicologie* 72, no. 2
        (1986): 277–282.

        A summary of the conference held in Warsaw, October 17–23,
1986. Provides a brief synopsis of the papers presented.

40.   Burhardt, Stefan. *Polonez: katalog tematyczny* 3 (1831–1981).
        Kraków: Polskie Wydawnictwo Muczyne, 1985. 818 p.   ISBN
        8322402465

        Chopin, items 93–111; pages 111–157.
        Lists Chopin polonaises with an incipit of the music. Provides
manuscript information and a list of editions. The volume contains plates
of some prints and manuscripts.

41.   Turner, J. Rigbie. "Nineteenth-Century Autograph Music Manu-
        scripts in the Pierpont Morgan Library. A Check List." *19th Cen-
        tury Music* 4, no. 1 (1980): 49–69.

        Lists the Chopin manuscripts in the collection with references to
the Brown and Kobylańska catalogs. Provides information on thirteen
manuscript works and seven letters. The collection includes the manuscripts collected by Cortot. Gives the background of the Chopin collections on deposit in the library.

PERIODICALS

Several periodicals are devoted exclusively to work on Chopin or to related topics and include frequent articles on the composer and his music.
Other serials have published special commemorative issues during anniversary years related to Chopin's birth (1910, 1960) or death (1949,
1989).

42.   *Neue Zeitschrift für Musik* 121, no. 3 (March 1960).

        Addresses the issues of editions and current research on Chopin.

43.   *Musical America* 49, no. 3 (February 1949).

        Special Chopin issue.

44. *Revue musicale* 12 no. 121 (December 1931).

A special edition devoted to Chopin. Contains contributions by many of the Chopin scholars active in the first half of the twentieth century. Articles cover Chopin's life, his music, and activities in Paris.

45. *Revue de musicologie* 75, no. 2 (1989).

Devoted to Chopin articles in anniversary of his death.

46. *Rocznik Chopinowski/Annales Chopin.* ML 410.C54 R55

Annales Chopin 2 (1957) contains some of the articles from *Rocznik Chopinowski* in French, German, or Russian translation.

47. *Rocznik Chopinowski* 19 (1987).

Contains proceedings of the International Musicological Symposium on Chopin and Romanticism, Warsaw, 17–23 October 1986. The volume includes plates of manuscripts and other iconographic relics bound into the center.

48. Nowik, Wojciech. "The Chopin Annual: History and Future." *Polish Music* 18, no. 1–2 (1983): 37–42.

Describes the purpose of *Rocznik Chopinowski* as a forum for Poland and Chopin scholars from around the world. Gives a history of the publication and a review of the contents over the years.

49. *Courrier musical* 13, no. 1 (1910).

An issue devoted to Chopin. Includes articles on Chopin's life, his genius, influences, and impressions of his music.

50. *Revue musicale* 1955 no. 229

Articles of a number of authors. Contributions relate to a chronology of Chopin's life, a history of the correspondence (a contribution by Sydow from the recently published editions of letters), the Delfina letters, and a list of Chopin portraits.

51. *Muzyka* 4, no. 4 (1959).

Issue devoted to articles on Chopin. Papers on Chopin's style and comparisons to the work of other composers. Abstracts in German.

52.   *Piano Quarterly* 29, no. 113 (Spring 1981).

       A special edition devoted Chopin. See 231.

53.   *Musica* 14, no. 3 (1960).

       Issue devoted to Frederic Chopin and Hugo Wolf.

54.   *Journal of the American Liszt Society.*

55.   Frederick Chopin Society. *Chopin Studies.* Warsaw, 1985–.
       ML 410.C54 C48   ISSN 0239–8567

Review: Jitka Ludvova, *Hudební veda* 24, no. 1 (1987): 95–96;
Arnfried Edler, *Die Musikforschung* 41, no. 2 (1988): 188–189.

Translations into English of previously published material from
the journal *Rocznik Chopinowski* (see 46) or conference papers. Kornel
Michałowski provides a classified bibliography of Chopin material with
an index. Additional articles include reviews of books and recordings.
Another book series published by Cambridge University Press shares the
same title (see 299–300).

RELATED CULTURAL HISTORY

A number of references can be provided to supplement the cultural background of Chopin's musical life. Provided are references on music in
nineteenth-century Warsaw and the broad view of nineteenth-century
Paris. Related topics might be the nineteenth-century salon culture and
technical information on piano manufacturing during the period.

56.   Davies, Norman. *God's Playground: A History of Poland.* New
       York: Columbia University Press, 1982. 2 vols. ISBN
       0231043260   DK 4140.D38

       Reviews: Stanisław Barańczak, *New Republic* 187 (November
15, 1982): 25; Leszek Kolakowski, *New York Times Book Review* (April
15, 1982): 6; Martin Malia, *New York Review of Books* 30 (September 29,
1983): 18; Ronald Modras, *America* 147 (December 18, 1982): 2; Olga
A. Norkiewicz, *History* 68 (1983): 126; Hugh Seton-Watson, *Times Literary Supplement* (March 19, 1982): 297; Piotr Wandycz, *American Historical Review* 80 (April 1983): 437; *Economist* 282 (March 6, 1982): 104.

Offers a comprehensive survey in English that is meant to be impartial and without an idealogical agenda. Takes a different approach to the issue of Polish nationalism than native scholars. Intersperses chronology with extracts from historical documents and references to cultural history, making the book more enjoyable to read than most historical surveys. Provides many plates of key Polish art works, maps of regions under discussion, and a good index.

57. Chechlińska, Zofia. "Badań Chopinowskie Zofii Lissy [Zofia Lissa's Research on Chopin]. *Rocznik Chopinowski* 13 (1981): 13–18.

Provides a biography with musicological activities of Lissa and notes the place of Chopin research in her career. Lissa's interests were the place of Chopin in music history and comparisons of Chopin's musical style with that of other composers.

58. Chrościcki, Juliusz A. and Andrzej Rottermund. *Atlas of Warsaw's Architecture.* Warsaw: Arkady Publishers, 1977. 248 p. NA 1455.P62 W762713

Reviews the development of Warsaw's architecture chronologically. The larger part of the book is a catalog of buildings sorted by street. Several references are made to sites associated with Chopin.

59. Kesting, Jürgen. "Salon—Thesen zu einem gesellschaftlichen Ort der Musik im 19. Jahrhundert." *Musik und Bildung* 9, no. 7–8 (1977): 377–380.

Begins with Schumann's references to Chopin waltzes as Salonmusik. Discusses implications of this term for politics, subjectivity, virtuosity, socialization, and the history of ideas.

60. Lissa, Zofia. "La musique en Pologne." In *La musique, les instruments, les oeuvres,* ed. Norbert Dufourq, II, 241–250. Paris: Librarie Larousse, 1965. 2 vols. 391, 399 pp.   ML 160.D782

Presents Chopin as a representative of romanticism who appealed to the national conscience of all independence movements. Concentrates on Chopin and the Polish national style. Gives related notes about Polish music, especially influences on musical style. Sketches the life and works of other nineteenth- and twentieth-century composers. This music encyclopedia is intended for a general audience and is well illustrated.

61.   Lissa, Zofia. "Klavierpolonaise und -mazurka im 19. Jahrhundert." In *Gattungen der Musik in Einzeldarstellungen,* ed. Wolf Arlt, Ernst Lichtenhahn and Hans Oesch, 813–839. Bern: Francke Verlag, 1973. 895 pp.   ML 55.S375 v. 1

Begins with a general discussion of the genres and the sources of the dances. Explores the polonaise before Chopin, Chopin's contribution, and his successors using musical examples. Considers the different types of mazurka rhythms. Provides information about other European composers writing in these genres.

62.   Łobaczewska, Stefania. "La culture musicale en Pologne au début du XIXe siècle et ses relations avec la musque de Chopin." In *The Book of the First Musicological Congress Devoted to the Works of Frederick Chopin,* ed. Zofia Lissa, 63–72. See 493.

Reviews Polish research on music of the first decades of the nineteenth century. The principal barrier to research is the state of musical monuments of the period. Examines assumptions concerning the origin of Chopin's style. Considers the roles of other composers and Polish folklore, especially with the mazurkas and polonaises.

63.   Martens, Heinrich, ed. "Polonaise und Mazurka," vol. 19 of *Muzikalische Formen in historischen Reihen.* Berlin-Lichterfelde: C.F. Vieweg, 1936. 20 vols.   MT 58.M36 M9

Gives an introductory essay with musical examples on the dances, especially the rhythms. Musical scores provide examples of polonaises and mazurkas before and after Chopin. Considers both Polish sources and the works of other European composers.

64.   Swartz, Anne. "Maria Szymanowska and the Salon Music of the Early Nineteenth Century." *Polish Review* 30, no. 1 (1985): 43–58.

Critically reviews the details of Szymanowska's life. Discusses her music through musical examples. Szymanowska preceeded Chopin in the compositions of etudes, preludes, mazurkas, polonaises, and nocturnes for piano.

65. Vogel, Beniamin. "Fortepiany i idiofony klawiszowe w Królestwie Polskim w latach młodości Chopina" [Pianos and keyboard idiophones in the Polish Kingdom in Chopin's youth]. *Rocznik Chopinowski* 9 (1975): 38–69.

Discusses pianos and other keyboard instruments in the period 1815–1830. Relates manufacturing and sales of instruments to the economy and political situation in Poland. Information gleaned from newspaper research. Lists piano makers in nineteenth-century Poland and Chopin's pianos.

CHAPTER 3

Life of the Composer

Biographies of Chopin have proliferated since the composer's death, each generation reinterpreting the known facts of his life and activities. An important source in all biographies is the correspondence. Misinformation and conjecture included in early biographies were adopted uncritically by later writers, and it is only in the more recent volumes that Polish sources have been widely consulted to illuminate Chopin's early period. Chopin's introspective music, his reserved nature, and relations with many artists of his time have all contributed to a life story that has stimulated the imagination. Not surprisingly, interpretation of the narrative has changed over the years in a manner not unlike variations among pianists in the interpretation of his music.

66. Liszt, Franz. *Frederic Chopin.* Trans. Edward N. Waters. London: Free Press, 1963. 184 p.   ML 410.C54 L734

This early biography of Chopin underscores the Polish roots of Chopin and their influence in his life. The warm friendship between Liszt and Chopin is also in evidence. Nevertheless, the book is believed to have been penned by Princess Carolyne von Sayn-Wittgenstein, Liszt's companion who was of Polish descent.

67. Sowinski, Albert. "Chopin." In *Les musiciens polonais et slaves. Dictionnaire biographique,* 113–122. Paris, 1857. Reprint, New York: Da Capo, 1971. 600 p.   ISBN 0306701669   ML 106.P7 S7

Comments on the composer's celebrity and character. Cites his ability at orchestration and the poetry of his music. Provides basic biographical information. Quotes Franz Liszt on Chopin's death. Includes a list of works. The book also contains entries on a number of contemporaries of Chopin and persons tied to his life.

68. Tarnowski, Stanislas. *Chopin: As Revealed by Extracts from His Diary.* Trans. Natalie Janotha. London: William Reeves, n.d. 70 p.   ML 410.C54 T2

Notes from lectures given in Krakow in 1871. No references to sources of information. Contains annotated comments from Chopin's journal.

69. Audley, A. *Frédéric Chopin: sa vie et ses oeuvres.* Paris: E. Plon, 1880. 245 p.

Gives the story of Chopin's life and travels. The final chapter addresses miscellaneous topics, including Chopin's students. Relies on quotations from letters, especially letters of other composers and musicians. Mentions names of contemporaries and Chopin's musical compositions throughout the biography. Includes a list of works.

70. Karasowski, Moritz. *Frederic Chopin: His Life and Letters.* Trans. Emily Hill. 3rd ed. London: William Reeves, 1938. Reprint, Westport, Conn.: Greenwood Press, 1970. 479 p. Originally published Dresden, 1872.   ML 410.C54 K3

Biography relies heavily on letters. Appendix prints letters to Wojciech Grzymała from 1845–1849, giving the Polish original and English translation on facing pages.

71. Niecks, Frederick. *Frederick Chopin as a Man and Musician.* New York: Cooper Square Publishers, 1973. 2 vols. Originally published in 1902.   ISBN 0815404786   ML 410.C54 N4 1973

Preface reviews the early historiography of research on Chopin from the Liszt biography. Gives some information about Poland, its literature, folk traditions, and social life. Outlines the activities of music and musicians in Poland before and during Chopin's lifespan. Incorporates a chapter on George Sand. Reconsiders Karasowski's dating of Chopin correspondence and exercises some caution in interpreting letters as a part of the biography. Appendices include an essay on the history of Polish music, short recollections of Chopin by others that expand comments in the text, a list of works with remarks, and a name index.

72.   Hunecker, James. *Chopin: The Man and His Music*. New York: Charles Scribners' Sons, 1900. Reprint, New York: Dover, 1966. 239 p.   ML 410.C54 P7

Short biography built on the work of Niecks (see 71). Tries to probe into Chopin's character, both the positive and negative traits. Considers Chopin as both a poet and psychologist in his music. Reviews the music, referring to other authors' comments about individual pieces. Provides bibliography.

73.   Pourtales, Guy de. *Polonaise: The Life of Chopin*. Trans. Charles Bayly, Jr. New York: Henry Holt, 1927. 349 p.   ML 410.C54 P7

Relates a romantic view of Chopin's life. Includes an index and short bibliography.

74.   Leichtentritt, Hugo. *Frédéric Chopin*. Berlin: Harmonie, 1905. 144 p.   ML 410.C54 L3

Refers to Niecks (see 71) as the standard biography. Discusses compositions by genre in sections separate from biography. Relies on excerpts from the letters. Uses short musical examples to support descriptive analyses of specific works. Illustrations appear throughout the text.

75.   Hoesick, Ferdynand. *Chopin. Życie i twórczość* [Chopin: Life and works]. Kraków: Polskie Wydawnictwo Muzyczne, 1962–1967. Biblioteka Chopinowska 5. 405, 452, 318, 453 p. Originally published Warszawa: Księgarki F. Hoesicka, 1927.   ML 410.C54 H632

An extended biography of Chopin. Gives good attention to the Polish period and cultural background. Some discussion of the music, but no musical examples. Includes an index and numerous illustrations.

76.   Ganche, Édouard. *Frédéric Chopin, sa vie et ses oeuvres 1810–1849*. 2nd ed. Paris: Mercure de France, 1949. 341 p. Reprint of 1913 edition, 1972.   ML 410.C54 G2 1972

The biography provides long exerpts from letters. Mentions compositions chronologically, but there is no analytical discussion of the music. The final chapter continues narrative after Chopin's death. Includes a bibliography and list of works.

77.   Scharlett, Bernard. *Chopin*. Leipzig: Breitkopf und Härtel, 1919.
       289 p.   ML 410.C54 A215

Covers the events of Chopin's life. Includes a chapter on
Chopin's general character. Discusses his works by genre incorporating
some musical examples, but mostly incipits. Includes a name index.

78.   Bidou, Henri. *Chopin*. Trans. Catherine Alison Phillips. New York:
       Knopf, 1931. 267 p. Originally published Paris: Felix Alcan, 1925.
       ML 410.C54 B531 1927

A biography of Chopin with some discussion of his music in-
serted into the narrative of his life. Provides short musical examples.
Makes reference to letters, concerts, and contemporary musical events.
Includes a list of works and a bibliography.

79.   Umińska, Zofia and H.E. Kennedy. *Chopin: The Child and the
       Lad*. London: Methuen, 1925. 91 p.   ML 410.C54 U6

Biographical information is limited to Chopin's childhood. The
facts of his life are greatly elaborated into a narrative.

80.   Dry, Wakeling. *Chopin*. London: John Lane the Bodley Head,
       1926. 118 p.   ML 410.C54 D79 1926

A short chronology of events in Chopin's life. Provides also a
survey of his music. Approach to Chopin is summarized by the following
quote: "His sentimental delicacy, wrought to an acute point by reason of
his illness, makes him the most artistic of the Romanticists." Covers the
music by genre, providing a description. Incorporates a few short musical examples.

81.   Binental, Leopold. *Chopin*. Leipzig: Breitkopf und Härtel, 1932.
       196 p.   ML 410.C54 B6

Provides an introduction to Chopin's life and the reception history of his music. Assesses his musical achievement. Includes many illustrations (110 plates) of portraits, manuscripts, printed compositions,
and correspondence. Gives notes on the photographic reproductions.

82. Maine, Basil. *Chopin.* New York: A.A. Wyn, 1949. 128 p. ML410.C54 M29

A short, popular "pocket" biography. Contains a concise list of works and bibliography. Concise descriptions of music are inserted into biographical narrative.

83. Hadden, J. Cuthbert. *Chopin.* Rev. ed. London: J.M. Dent, 1934. Reprint, New York: AMS, 1977. 243 p.   ML 410.C54 H2 1934

Review: David Zakeri Kushner, *Journal of the American Liszt Society* 11 (June 1982): 77–79.
Mostly a biography of the composer. A separate chapter assesses "the man, teacher, player, and composer." Gives scant information on the Polish period. Discusses the music in one chapter.

84. Murdock, William. *Chopin: His Life.* New York: Macmillan, 1935. 410 p.

This biography relies on the Chopin correspondence for much of its information. Provides a list of published works, bibliography, and index.

85. Hedley, Arthur. *Chopin.* Rev. ed. London: J.M. Dent, 1974. 214 p.   ML 410.C54 H3 1974

Biography of the composer relying on quotations from his letters. Addresses misunderstandings and misinformation as found in earlier biographies. Examines music separately from life with chapters organized by genre. Provides a chronology of life events, catalog of works, and a short bibliography. A "Personalia" identifies persons named in the text.

86. Gide, André. *Notes sur Chopin.* Paris: L'Arche, 1948. 115 p.

87. Gide, André. *Notes on Chopin.* Trans. Bernard Frechtman. New York: Philosophical Library, 1949. 126 p. Reprint, Westport, Conn.: Greenwood Press, 1978.   ISBN 0313203717   ML 410.C54 G53

Review: Hanno Ehrler, *Neue Zeitschrift für Musik* 150, no. 9 (Sept 1989): 52.
Notes or impressions about the interpretation of Chopin's music using examples from specific pieces. Provides a descriptive review of pieces. Quotes fragments from Chopin's journal that relate to music in general as well as specific compositions. Includes a letter from M. Ed. Ganche in response to Gide's book.

88.   Mizwa, Stephen P. *Frederic Chopin 1810–1849.* New York:
       Macmillan for the Kościuszko Foundation, 1949. 108 p. Reprint,
       Westport, Conn.: Greenwood Press, 1983.   ISBN 0313241163
       ML 410.C54 F74

       Essays cover Chopin's role in the history of Polish music and the
American events of the Chopin centennial. Addresses the role of Delfina
Potocka in Chopin's life. Uses excerpts from letters in the section ex-
plaining Chopin's thoughts on music and other musicians (written by
Sydow).

89.   Wierzynski, Casimir. *The Life and Death of Chopin.* New York:
       Simon and Schuster, 1949. 444 p.   ISBN 671209108   ML
       410.C54 W5

90.   Wierzyński, Kazimierz. *Życie Chopina* [The life of Chopin].
       Kraków: Wydawnictwo Literackie, 1978. 380 p.   ML 410.C54
       W57

       Begins with the arrival of Nicolas Chopin in Poland. Relies on
quotations for the letters. Contrary to the English title, the book does not
dwell on the death of the composer. Short review of events and reactions
after his death, including the issue of letters to Delfina. Bibliography,
index.

91.   Czech, Stany. *Chopin. Erdenweg eines Genius.* Hattingen, Ger-
       many: Hundt-Verlag, 1950. 344 p.   ML 410.C54 C95

       The biography underscores the reception of Chopin's work. No
use of musical examples to discuss music. Provides a short bibliography
and list of works. The name index (pages 301–344) identifies persons
tangentially connected to Chopin's activities.

92.   Bory, Robert. *La vie de Frédéric Chopin par l'image.* Paris:
       Horizons de France, 1949. 218 p.   ML 88.C46 B67

       A biographical sketch accompanies reproductions of Chopin and
other figures associated with his life. Also provides plates of selected letters, manuscripts of compositions, title pages of printed music, and concert programs.

93.   Broszkiewicz, Jerzy. *Kształt miłości* [The form of love].
       Warszawa: Spółdzielnia Wydawnicza "Czytelnik," 1953. 423 p.
       ML 410.C54 B888

The story of Chopin's life fictionalized. Weaves the standard
facts of his life into the narrative.

94.   Jachimecki, Zdzisław. *Chopin: Rys życia i twórczości* [Chopin:
       features of his life and works]. Kraków: Polskie Wydawnictwo
       Muzyczne, 1957. 337 p.   ML 410.C54 J14

Taken from early biographies and correspondence. Concentrates
on Chopin's performance career and creative life. Discusses the music
by genre. Includes a bibliography.

95.   Czartkowski, Adam and Zofia Jeżewska. *Chopin Żywy.* [Chopin
       living]. Warszawa: Państwowy Instytut Wydawniczy, 1959. 614 p.
       ML 410.C54 C93

A biography addressing Chopin's artistic life. Tends to be balanced
more toward the early Polish period. Broadens the sources of information on Chopin beyond the correspondence. Includes a bibliography
and index.

96.   Belza, Igor'. *Friderik Franchishek Shopen* [F. F. Chopin].
       Moskva: Izdatel'stvo Akademii Nauk SSSR, 1960. 462 p.   ML
       410.C54 B29

Concentrates on the Warsaw period in Chopin's life and his early
musical training. Discusses the music alongside biographical details referring to specific musical examples. Uses newspaper references as documentation. Later periods in Chopin's life are approached through the
ballades, preludes, sonatas, and polonaises.

97.   Bourniquel, Camille. *Chopin.* Trans. Sinclair Road. Evergreen
       Profile Books, 8. New York: Grove Press, 1960. 191 p.   ML
       410.C54 B732

A short biography that attempts to dispell the mythological romantic view of Chopin's life. Nationalism is viewed as Chopin's burden.
For a popular book in paperback, it includes many plates and illustrations. Places the events of the composer's life in historical and cultural
context. Several chapters are devoted to music, with the discussion organized by genre. Addresses Italian influences in a separate chapter. In-

cludes a bibliography and discography of sources from Great Britain and the United States.

98.   Glinski, Matteo. *Chopin the Unknown.* Windsor, Ontario: Assumption University of Windsor Press, 1963. 84 p.   ML 410.C54 G63

Illuminates Chopin's secret religious and spiritual life. Provides a chronology of the composer's life concentrating on spirituality. Focuses on the nocturnes as the reflection of this spirituality in his music.

99.   Grenier, Jean-Marie. *Frédéric Chopin.* Paris: Pierre Seghers, 1964. 182 p.   ML 410.C54 G75

About half of this popular work is a short biography. Musical works are addressed individually with short descriptions. One section of the book is devoted to quotations from Chopin's contemporaries. Includes a list of works, discography, and illustrations.

100.   Weinstock, Herbert. *Chopin: The Man and His Music.* New York: Alfred A. Knopf, 1969. Reprint, New York: Da Capo, 1981. 336 p.   ISBN 0306760819   ML 410.C54 W26

The biography considers critically prior writing on the composer, carefully using the correspondence and other evidence to determine the events in the composer's life. The review of Chopin's music proceeds by opus number and is supported by musical examples. Includes a bibliography and indexes.

101.   Belotti, Gastone. *F. Chopin l'uomo.* Sapere Edizioni, 1974. 3 vols. 1632 p.   ML 410.C54 B24

A well-documented biography drawing on the Chopin letters and other research. Gives extended quotations from the correspondence. Does not discuss music in depth. Includes extensive indexes.

102.   Orga, Ateş. *Chopin: His Life and Times.* New York: Midas Books, 1976. Rev. ed. Tunbridge Wells: Midas, 1978. 144 p.   ISBN 0859360571   ML 410.C54 O73

Review: Dalila Turło, *Rocznik Chopinowski* 13 (1981): 159–166.
Biography with no discussion of Chopin's music. Incorporates many plates and illustrations. Provides some quotations from letters. Includes an index and short bibliography.

103. Dułęba, Władysław. *Chopin.* Kraków: Polskie Wydawnictwo Muzyczne, 1975. 304 p.   ML 410.C54 D84

A biography written in Polish and intended as a popular work with many illustrations and reproductions. Includes short quotations from letters. No detailed discussion of music.

104. Gavoty, Bernard. *Frederic Chopin.* Trans. Martin Sokolinsky. New York: Charles Scribners Sons, 1977. 452 p.   ISBN 0684149303 ML 410.C54 G2753

Review: Zygmunt Mycielski, *Rocznik Chopinowski* 10 (1978): 69–71.

Gives attention to both the Polish period in Chopin's life and his time in France. Expands the biography with background information. Uses quotations from letters, journals, and contemporary documents. Discusses the musical works in separate chapter, with general comments about each genre. Includes an index and chronological table of life and works.

105. Marek, George R. and Maria Gordon-Smith. *Chopin.* London: Weidenfeld and Nicolson, 1978. 289 p.   ISBN 0297776169 ML 410.C54 M37

Review: Jeffrey Kallberg, *Notes* 36, no. 3 (March 1980): 645– 646.

Biography that stresses the Polish cultural background and attempts to add objectivity about the role of Poland in Chopin's life. Not a treatise on Chopin's music. Biography relies on quotations from letters and newspaper articles. Includes a bibliography and chronology. The appendix reports on the letters to Delfina.

106. Jordan, Ruth. *Nocturne: A Life of Chopin.* New York: Taplinger, 1978. 286 p.   ISBN 0800855930   ML 410.C54 J85 1978

Reviews: Dalila Turło, *Rocznik Chopinowski* 13 (1981): 159– 166; Alan Walker, *Music and Letters* 60, no. 3 (July 1979): 361–362; Robert L. Jacobs, *Music Review* 40, no. 3 (August 1979): 217–218; Jeffrey Kallberg, *Notes* 36, no. 3 (March 1980): 645–646.

A narrative account of Chopin's life. Includes the letters to Delfina as evidence, despite the controversy of their authenticity, and modifies the view of Chopin's life accordingly. The book includes a bibliography and is indexed.

107.   Zamoyski, Adam. *Chopin: A New Biography*. Garden City, N.Y.: Doubleday, 1980. 374 p.   ISBN 0385135971.   ML 410.C54 Z33 1980

Adds detailed information on the cultural background of Poland to the story of Chopin's life. Sorts some of the myths about the composer. Supports the biography with references to Chopin's correspondence. Addresses Chopin's relationship with Delfina Potocka. Mentions the musical works for their historical context, but does not discuss the music in detail. Includes a list of works, list of sources, and an essay on the Delfina Potocka correspondence.

108.   Atwood, William G. *The Lioness and the Little One: The Liaison of George Sand and Frederic Chopin*. New York: Columbia University Press, 1980. 316 p.   ISBN 0231049420   PQ 2414.A8

Review: Jeffrey Kallberg, *19th Century Music* 5, no. 3 (Spring 1982): 244–246.
Tells the story of this nine-year relationship. Considers individual strengths and flaws, both human and artistic. The material is mostly drawn from correspondence; excerpts from letters are inserted into the narrative. Chopin's music is not discussed. Plates of relevant people and places are printed in the book, including exterior and interior photographs of Nohant.

109.   Atwood, William G. *Fryderyk Chopin: Pianist from Warsaw*. New York: Columbia University Press, 1987. 305 p.   ISBN 02131064063   ML 410.C54 A77

Review: Thomas Higgins, *Journal of Musicological Research* 8, no. 3–4 (March 1989): 359–398; Geraldine Keeling, *Journal of the American Liszt Society* 24 (July-December 1988): 109–112; Charles Rosen, *New York Review of Books* 34, no. 9 (May 1987): 9–11; Anne Swartz, *Polish Review* 32, no. 3 (1987): 319–320.
Organizes Chopin's life by place and time, placing an emphasis on the musical life of each location. The book is especially good in presenting the musical life of Warsaw in the nineteenth century. Appendices provide a list of concerts and concert reviews. The book addresses cultural history more than analysis of Chopin's music.

110. Zieliński, Tadeusz Andrzej. *Chopin: Życie i droga twórcza* [Chopin: Life and the path of creation]. Kraków: Polskie Wydawnictwo Muzyczne, 1993. 666 p.

Discusses the composer's stylistic development throughout the course of this biography by integrating the discussion of the music with the facts of Chopin's life. Considers the stages of artistic development. Gives some analysis of music supported with musical examples. Includes a name index and index of references to Chopin works. Notes reconcile contradicting facts of earlier biographers.

111. Siepmann, Jeremy. *Chopin: The Reluctant Romantic*. Boston: Northeastern University Press, 1995. 280 p. ISBN 1555532497 ML 410.C54S58 1995

Biography of the composer intended to incorporate the research of the previous twenty years. Aimed between the fanciful biographical writings and detailed musicological studies. Contains general commentary on musical genres. Short essays on genres are formated as interludes and placed between chapters of biography. Includes illustrations, bibliography, discography, a chronology of events in Chopin's life with world and artistic events, and notes on personalities encountered in the text.

112. Temperly, Nicolas. "Fryderyk Chopin," In *The New Grove Early Romantic Masters 1, Chopin, Schumann, Liszt*, pp. 1–96. New York: Norton, 1985. ML 390.E277 1995 v. 1

Covers biographical data on the composer, his compositional style, and historical position. Provides a detailed list of works. An extensive bibliography compiled by Kornel Michałowski is included.

Several research studies focus on specific aspects of Chopin's life, such as his health, travels, and relationships.

113. Belotti, Gastone. "Okoliczności powstania pierwszej monografii o Chopinie" [The circumstances of the making of the first monograph about Chopin]. *Rocznik Chopinowski/Annales Chopin* 7 (1965–1968): 7–33.

Reviews what is known about the creation of Liszt's biography of Chopin, including Liszt's friendship with Chopin. Refers to *Lucrezia Floriani* for information on Chopin's character. Considers Liszt's motivation for working on the biography and speculates on relationships within the Chopin-Sand circle. Assesses the usefulness of the Liszt biography as a historical document.

114. Belotti, Gastone. "Problemi e limiti di una biografia di Chopin." In *Chopin in Italia,* pp. 3–64. Wrocław: Zakład Narodowy imienia Ossolińskich Wydawnictwo PAN, 1977. Accademia Polacca delle Scienze, Conferenze e Studi, 72. ML 410.C54 B23

Reviews the source materials for a definitive biography of Chopin. Covers the work to date on Chopin biography and considers interpretive problems.

115. *Chopin in Silesia.* Katowice, 1974. Fascicles of the Archives "Music Culture in Silesia," Music College Library, Katowice, no. 1. 24 p. ML 410.C54 C4673

A pamphlet of research papers exploring Chopin's connections with Silesia and to other musicians from the region. Contributions address Chopin's relationship with Józef Elsner and the sites Wrocław, Cieszyń, and Duszniki.

116. Gawroński, Ludwik. "Tytus Woyciechowski—Przyjaciel Chopina" [T. Woyciechowski—Friend of Chopin]. *Ruch Muzyczny* 19, no. 21 (November 12, 1975): 4–6.

Reviews existing information about Woyciechowski. Makes reference to the correspondence.

117. Gurewicz, Sergiusz. "Miał wyostrzoną wrażliwość—o niektórych właściwościach choroby Fryderika Chopina" [About some characteristics of the illness of F. Chopin]. *Ruch Muzyczny* 23, no. 21 (October 21, 1979): 18–19.

Introduces a psychic perspective into the diagnosis of Chopin's illness. Evidence is found in the emotional state of his music and comments in letters.

118. Hedley, Arthur. "Some Notes on Chopin Biography." *Music and Letters* 18, no. 1 (January 1937): 42–49.

Comments on published biographies of Chopin. Niecks (71) omitted Polish sources, particularly F. Hoesick's *Chopin,* (1911; 3 vols.).

Hoesick is cited in Niecks bibliography, but not consulted. Hedley relates information on the early Polish period of Chopin.

119. Harasowski, Adam. *The Skein of Legends Around Chopin.* Glasgow: William MacLellan, 1967. Reprint, New York: Da Capo Press, 1980. 417 p. ISBN 0306775255 ML 410.C54 H25

Reviews many of the Chopin biographies, beginning with the book by Liszt. Gives detailed critical assessments. Discusses the attraction of Chopin's life in light of its many mysteries. Addresses the issue of the Delfina correspondence. Reprints articles originally published in *Music and Musicians* (February 1969 and March 1973). See 160.

120. Jeżewska, Zofia. *Chopin w kraju rodzinnym* [Chopin in his native land]. Warszawa: Wydawnictwo PTTK „Kraj," 1985. 151 p. ML 410.C54 J48 1985

Gives historical background to all the sites visited by Chopin in Poland. Provides descriptions and background to the current Chopin monuments. The biography of Chopin's Polish period includes references to the places that his family lived. Includes many historical illustrations. Summaries in English, French, German, and Russian.

121. Jüttner, Karl Richard. "Um Chopins Geburtsjahr." *Die Musikforschung* 7 (1954): 463–465.

Gives support for the date of March 1 as Chopin's birthday, following the view of Sydow. Provides evidence for the year of birth as 1809.

122. Jüttner, Karl Richard. "Chopins Vater." *Die Musikforschung* 10 (1957): 408–409.

Reviews what is known about Chopin's father and his family, particularly the move to Poland.

123. Kobylańska, Krystyna. "Chopin i Matuszyński: nieznane dokumenty" [Chopin and Matuszyński: Unknown Documents]. *Ruch Muzyczny* 23, no. 24 (December 2, 1979): 3–5.

Discusses marriage records of Matuszyński with Chopin's signature. Requires a reconsideration of the importance of Matuszyński in Chopin's life, despite limited mention in the correspondence.

124.   Lupack, Barbara T. "Chopin: New Biographical Insights." *Polish Review* 27, no. 1–2 (1982): 141–149.

A review article on Atwood, *Lioness and the Little One* (see 108) and Zamoyski, *Chopin* (107). Summarizes Chopin's life, noting each author's contribution to Chopin biography. Focuses on Chopin's relationships with people. No reference to specific musical works.

125.   Rambeau, Marie-Paule. *Chopin dans la vie et l'oeuvre de George Sand*. Paris: Société d'Édition des Belles Lettres, 1985. 393 p. ISBN 2251365265   PQ 2414.R36.1985

Strives to present a more complete view of the Chopin and Sand relationship. Compares and contrasts Chopin references in correspondence, memoirs, and works. Dispels the myths of their relationship and tackles issues such as Chopin's aesthetic taste and his progressive illness. Presents Sand's view of Chopin as an artist. Part II of the book places their relationship and art in historical context. Includes bibliography, indices, and chronology of the relationship 1838–1849.

126.   Ferrá, Bartolomé. *Chopin and George Sand in Majorca*. Trans. James Webb. Palma de Mallorca, 1936. Reprinted 1974.   ML 410.C54 F513

A more objective view of the Majorca trip, which gives the perspective of the natives. Makes references to the writings of George Sand.

127.   Franken, Franz Hermann. *Haydn, Beethoven, Bellini, Mendelssohn, Chopin, Schumann*. Vol. 1 of *Die Krankheiten grosser Komponisten*. Wilhelmshaven: Heinrichshofen, 1990. Taschenbücher der Musikwissenschaft. 3 vols. 303 p.   ISBN 3795904196   ML 390.F72K72

Review: Frieder Reininghaus, *Neue Zeitschrift für Musik* 148, no. 12 (December 1987): 70, 72.

Chopin is discussed on pages 189–237. Follows a biography format with the narrative focusing on Chopin's health at different stages in his life. Notes symptoms of tuberculosis from biographical evidence and family references. Includes sample plates of portraits and iconography.

128. Sielużycki, Czesław. "O zdrowiu Chopina. Prawdy, domniemania, legendy" [About Chopin's health: Truths, conjectures, legends]. *Rocznik Chopinowski* 15 (1983): 69–116.

An assessment of Chopin's health, much taken from the letters. Offers a list of Chopin's physicians.

129. Pistone, Danièle, ed. *Sur les traces de Frédéric Chopin.* Paris: Editions Champion, 1984. 312 p. ISBN 2852031337 ML 410.C54 S865 1984

Review: Irena Poniatowska, *Rocznik Chopinowski* 17 (1985): 253–262; Yves Lenoir, *Études classiques* 40, no. 3 (July 1987): 339.
Papers from a conference of May 7, 1983 held at the University of Paris-Sorbonne. Conference topics divided into three sections: the man and his mileux, works and his destiny, and the history of Chopin studies. All contributions published in French.

130. Ramero, Jesus C. *Chopin en Mexico.* México: Imprenta Universitaria, 1950. 83 p. ML 410.C54 R6

Discusses the introduction of Chopin's music to Mexico, focusing on performing artists and repertory. Covers events such as the Chopin celebrations.

131. Tomaszewska, Wanda. "Chopin w Dusznikach" [Chopin in Duszniki]. *Muzyka* 6, no. 4 (1961): 88–96.

Paints an image of Duszniki in the first half of the nineteenth century, focused on the cultural life of the town. Gives the details about Chopin's stay in Duszniki to cure his health in August of 1826. Covers activities and concerts. Considers the later circumstances around the construction of a monument to Chopin.

132. *Z zycia i twórzości Fryderyka Chopina* [From the life and works of F. Chopin]. *Kwartalnik Muzyczny* 7 (1949). 435 p.

Essays on Chopin's final days, unknown documents, specific works, and musical style. Bibliography of works related to Chopin from 1939–1949.

CORRESPONDENCE

The Chopin letters transmit the core of our understanding about the composer, his relations, and business dealings. The original language of the letters, primarily Polish and French, depends on Chopin's relationship with the correspondent. Although the major collections of Chopin letters have long ago been edited and published, recent discoveries have added to the corpus of correspondence.

133.   *Korespondencja Fryderyka Chopina* [Correspondence of F. Chopin]. Ed. Bronisław Edward Sydow. Warszawa: Państwowy Instytut Wydawniczy, 1955. 2 vols. 604 p.   ML 410.C54 A 283

A collection of 700 letters printed in the original Polish or Polish translation. The French texts are given in an appendix.

134.   *Correspondance de Frédéric Chopin.* Ed. Bronisław Edward Sydow. Paris: Richard-Masse, 1953–1960. 3 vols. 324, 416, 479 p. Reprint, Paris: Revue musicale, 1981.   ML 410.C54A283
        I.   L'aube 1816–1831, 324 p.
        II.   L'ascension, 1831–1840, 416 p.
        III. La gloire, 1840–1849, 479 p.

Review: Michael Stegemann, *Neue Zeitschrift für Musik* 146, no. 4 (April 1985): 57–58.
All letters are presented in French. Includes indices of names and places.

135.   Jachimecki, Zdzisław, ed. *Wybór listów* [Selected letters]. Wrocław: Wydawnictwo Zakładu Narodowego imienia Ossolińskich, 1949. 211 p.

Begins with an introduction about Chopin's life and works. Includes an essay on the publication and use of the correspondence. Prints 115 letters.

136.   Kukharskiĭ, F.S. *F. Shopen Pis'ma* [F. Chopin: Letters]. Moskva: Muzyka, 1976. 2 vols. 527, 468 p.

A Russian translation of the Chopin letters. Includes 832 items and some other documents. Provides a list of personages with notes on identity.

137. Kobylańska, Krystyna, ed. *Korespondencja Fryderyka Chopina z rodziną* [F. Chopin's correspondence with his family]. Warszawa: Państwowy Instytut Wydawniczy, 1972. 413 p.   ML 410.C54 A238

Letters between Chopin and family members, including his parents, sisters, and their families. Presents texts in Polish; letters of Chopin's father originally in French are given in an appendix. Other letters and documents also grouped in an appendix.

138. Kobylańska, Krystyna, ed. *Korespondencja Fryderyka Chopina z George Sand i z jej dziećmi* [Correspondence of F. Chopin with George Sand and her children]. Warszawa: Państowy Instytut Wydawniczy, 1981. 368 p.   ISBN 8306003268   ML 410.C54 A2823 1981

Begins with an introductory essay on the history of the letters and a chronological table of relationships. The letters, including those in other sources, are presented in the original and Polish translation. Notes to the letters give information on the first publication of each and current scholarship on dating. Reproductions of letters are included in the book.

139. *Selected Correspondence of Fryderyk Chopin, Abridged from Sydow.* Trans. and ed. Arthur Hedley. New York: McGraw-Hill, 1963. 400 p.   ML 410.C54 A2835 1979

In addition to translations of selected letters (see 133), includes a seven-page biographical summary of Chopin's life and a chronology. The Chopin-Potocki letters are treated in an essay from 1961, placed in an appendix. Includes an index of names and compositions.

140. *Chopin's Letters.* Ed. Henryk Opieński. Trans. E.L. Voynich. New York: Knopf, 1931. Reprint, New York: Dover, 1988. 424 p. ISBN 0486255646   ML 410.C54A4

An English translation of 294 selected letters. Includes an index of names cited.

141. Scharlitt, Bernard. *Friedrich Chopins gesammelte Briefe.* Leipzig: Breitkopf und Härtel, 1911. 305 p.   ML 410.C54 A215

Provides an introductory essay on the Chopin letters and correspondents. Contains 166 letters.

142.   Kobylańska, Krystyna. "Fryderyk Chopin. Miscellanea inedita."
        Ruch Muzyczny 40, no. 5 (10 March 1996): 32–37.

Gives information about unpublished letters: Chopin and George
Sand to Wojciech Grzymała (17 July 1843) and a letter of Grzymała to
Princess Anna Czartoryska. Reproduces documents.

143.   Kobylańska, Krystyna. "Fryderyk Chopin. Miscellanea inedita."
        Ruch Muzyczny 40, no. 8 (21 April 1996): 32–36.

Information on a letter of Chopin to Franchomme and a letter of
Marie de Rozières.

144.   Hordyński, Władysław. "Nieznany list Chopina do Teresa
        Wodzińskiej" [An unknown letter of Chopin to T. Wodzińska]. In
        *The Book of the First Musicological Congress Devoted to the
        Works of Frederick Chopin,* ed. Zofia Lissa, 675–678. See 493.

Discusses a letter from Chopin to Teresa Wodzińska from Paris
(23 September 1836) in answer to Wodzińska's letter (14 September
1836). Wodzińska further responded on 2 October 1836.

145.   Kasprzyk, Jerzy. "Pełny tekst listu Chopina do Ferdinanda
        Hillera" [The full text of a letter of Chopin to Ferdinand Hiller].
        Muzyka 21, no. 1 (1976): 111–117.

Reviews Chopin's contact with Hiller. Transcribes a letter of August 1832 in French. Reproduces plates of the original.

146.   Kossak, Ewa K. "O wydaniu korrespondencji George Sand—
        Georgesa Lubin" [The correspondence of George Sand—edited
        by Georges Lubin]. *Rocznik Chopinowski* 12 (1980): 11–39.

Reviews this edition of correspondence, focusing on Chopin.
Provides a fabric of names associated with Chopin's biography.

147.   Kobylańska, Krystyna. "Nieznane listy Fryderyka Chopina"
        [Unknown letters of Chopin]. *Ruch Muzyczny* 24, no. 14 (July 13,
        1980): 9–12.

Discusses gaps in the record of correspondence and that there are
few letters in some years. Presents ten unknown letters, most of which
are short notes of invitation or gratitude.

148. Kobylańska, Krystyna. "Odnaleziony list Chopina" [A discovered letter of Chopin]. *Ruch Muzyczny* 34, no. 26 (December 30, 1990): 1, 7.

Discusses a letter to Dr. Lyshinski dated November 3, 1848. Compares the letter to the version in the Sydow edition (see 133), but offers a different transcription from the manuscript.

149. Kobylańska, Krystyna. "Transkrypcje listów Chopina" [Transcriptions of Chopin's letters]. *Ruch Muzyczny* 16, no. 19 (October 1–15, 1972): 3–5.

Discusses mistakes in transcribing letters as published by Karasowski in *Fryderyk Chopin—Życie-listy-dzieła*. Traces the inconsistancies between published texts and copies of twenty letters received by TiFC in 1960 from Chopin's family.

150. *Deux lettres de Chopin au Chateau de Mariemont*. Ed. Ignace Blachman. Paris: Édition de l'Arche, 1949. 31 p.

Prints facsimiles of two Chopin letters written in French, and provides commentary placing the correspondence in context. A letter is to Józef Elsner (29 August 1826) and a card that mentions a sonata was written to an unknown addressee (1845).

151. Suttoni, Charles. "Liszt Correspondence in Print: An Expanded, Annotated Bibliography." *Journal of the American Liszt Society* 25 (January–June 1989): 1–157.

Publishes an annotated bibliography of letters and documents in collections and research articles. Gives cross references. The article is well indexed.

152. Wróblewska-Straus, Hanna. "Autografy Fryderyka Chopina ze zbiorów Muzeum TiFC w Warszawie. Suplement do katalogu" [Chopin autographs from the collections of the Chopin Society Museum in Warsaw. Catalog supplement]. *Rocznik Chopinowski* 14 (1982): 77–96.

Lists 24 items with a bibliography and index of related names. Provides plates of letters.

153. Wróblewska-Straus, Hanna. "Listy Jane Wilhelminy Stirling do Ludwiki Jędrzejewiczowej" [Jane Wilhelmina Stirling's letters to Ludwika Jędrzejewicza]. *Rocznik Chopinowski* 12 (1980): 55–193.

Gives introductory information on 50 letters that span the years 1849–1854. Provides the original French text with Polish translation. Footnotes provide explanatory information. A chart tabulates published versions of the letters in editions by M. Karłowicz, E. Ganche, and A.E. Bone, some in fragments. The article concludes with complete indices and a bibliography. Several plates of manuscript pages are bound into the journal.

154. Wróblewska-Straus, Hanna. "'Kochany Delacroix list Ci ode mnie duży zawiezie' Korespondencja Fryderyka Chopina z Wojciechem Grzymałą" ["Dear Delacroix, your letter to me conveys much." The correspondence of F. Chopin with Wojciech Grzymała]. *Ruch Muzyczny* 24, no. 13 (June 29, 1980): 16–18.

Discusses letters in the Biblioteka Czartoryski in Kraków, particularly a letter of 30 August 1846 from Chopin to Grzymała. Transcribes the letter and places it in context. Reproduction of document.

155. Wróblewska-Straus, Hanna. "Nowe Chopiniana w zbiorach Towarzystwa im. Fryderyka Chopina" [New Chopin memorabilia in the collections of the Chopin Society]. *Rocznik Chopinowski* 8 (1969): 125–145.

Provides information on letters of Chopin to Julian Fontana (October 1836–1837), Fontana to Ludwika Jędrzejewicza (February 2, 1852), I. Barcińska to Schlesinger (February 9, 1857), I. Bacińska (August 3, 1857), Jules Janina to Chopin (1835–1836), and a letter to Maurice Sand (1844). Transcribes the text of the letters.

156. Wróblewska-Straus, Hanna. "'Precz z oczu moich.' Nowe autografy Fryderyka Chopina w zbiorach TiFC" ["Out of my sight." New autographs of F. Chopin in the collections of the Chopin Society]. *Ruch Muzyczny* 20, no. 21 (October 10, 1976): 3–5.

157. Wróblewska-Straus, Hanna. "Korespondencja Chopina jego przyjaciół i znajomych oraz omowienie wpływów Muzealnych

Towarzystwa im. Fryderyka Chopina w Warszawie" [Correspondence of Chopin and his friends, as well as discussion of influences in the Chopin Society Museum in Warsaw]. *Rocznik Chopinowski* 21 (1995):

Discusses Chopin letters available through recent auctions. Fourteen letters of Chopin, George Sand, and others are transcribed. The French language letters are translated into Polish. The original language is provided and extensive footnotes document the context of the correspondence. Includes facsimiles of the originals and a name index.

Given the importance of the Chopin correspondence to our understanding of the man and his music, it is understandable that the letters between Chopin and Delfina Potocka have been controversial. The letters were a discovery of post–World War II Poland, a time when the country was making a great effrot to identify and study its cultural artifacts. Due to both a lack of original manuscripts and unusual details of Chopin's relationship with Potocka, the authenticity of the letters has caused a lasting debate.

158. Gliński, Mateusz, ed. *Chopin. Listy do Delfiny* [Chopin: Letters to Delfina]. New York: Chopin Publishing Fund, 1972. 395 p.

Begins with a long introduction on Chopin's relationship with Potocka and the controversy of the letters. Publishes the texts of 122 letters. Extensive documentation in the form of footnotes is provided for the introduction and letters. The appendixes include documentation on the authenticity of the letters, illustrations of Potocka and documents related to the controversy, and a bibliography.

159. Czeczot, Zbigniew and Andrzej Zacharias. "Ekspertyza graficzno-porówawcza czterach fragmentów kwestionowanego pisma Fryderyka Chopina" [Expert handwriting analysis of four fragments of Chopin's questionable letters]. *Rocznik Chopinowski* 10 (1976–1977): 49–57.

Provides a handwriting analysis of four letters to Delfina Potocka. Discusses the authors' methodology and findings. The authors, members of the criminology department at Warsaw University, conclude that the analyzed letters are by Chopin. Includes plates of the handwriting samples.

160.   Harasowski, Adam. "Fact or Forgery." *Music and Musicians* 21,
        no. 7 (March 1973): 28–33.

Discusses the relative authenticity of the letter fragments to Delfina Potocka. Reviews the events in the controversy, especially the Hed-
ley-Glinski debate. Points to poor choices in translating the letters from
Polish and prints the most reliable translation into English of the Delfina
texts. Reprinted in 119.

161.   Higgins, Thomas. "Delphine Potocka and Frederic Chopin."
        Journal of the American Liszt Society 8 (1980): 64–74; 9 (1981):
        73–87.

Provides a synthesis of events in the controversy. Assesses the
role of key scholars in discussing the documentary evidence and gives a
personal role in communicating with other scholars on the Delfina issue.
Higgins hypothesizes that Delfina and Chopin had a discreet intimacy in
1832.

162.   Lissa, Zofia. "Chopins Briefe an Delfina Potocka." *Die Musik-
        forschung* 15 (1962): 341–353.

Reviews the discussion on the disputed letters to 1962, summa-
rizing arguments. Concentrates on the role of Paulina Czernicka in the
controversy.

163.   Lissa, Zofia. "O listach Fryderyka Chopina do Delfiny Potockiej"
        [About F. Chopin's letters to Delfina Potocka]. *Muzyka* 8, no. 1–2
        (1963): 110–126.

Reviews the origins of the Delfina controversy and early actions
of Pauline Czernicka. Discusses the authenticity of the letters and summarizes analyses of the contents of the letters.

164.   Soszalski, Ryszard and Władysław Wojcik. "Ekspertyza Nr
        ZKE-P-2871/74 w sprawie listów Fryderyka Chopina do Del-
        phiny Potockiej" [See next item]. *Rocznik Chopinowski* 10
        (1976–1977): 59–68.

165.   Soszalski, Ryszard and Władysław Wojcik. "Examination no.
        ZKE-P-2871–74 of Frederick Chopin's letters to Delfina Po-
        tocka." *Chopin Studies* 1 (1985): 165–172.

An analysis of the extant documents using criminal investigation
techniques.

166. Gliński, Mateusz. "Les lettres de Chopin à Delphine Potocki." In *The Book of the First Musicological Congress Devoted to the Works of Frederick Chopin,* ed. Zofia Lissa, pp. 669–674. See 493.

Relates the history of Chopin's correspondence and transmission of the letters. Presents reasons both for and against the authenticity of the Delfina letters.

167. Hedley, Arthur. "W sprawie fotografii rzekomych listów Chopina do Delphiny Potockiej" [In the matter of the photographs of the supposed letters of Chopin to D. Potocka]." *Ruch Muzyczny* 12, no. 6 (March 15–31, 1968): 15–16.

A response to Glinski regarding the photocopies of these controversial letters and their authenticity.

168. Nowik, Wojciech. "Spór Delfiński w latach ostatnich" [The Delfina debate in recent years]. *Rocznik Chopinowski* 12 (1980): 195–201.

Reviews the history of the Delfina issue, particularly controversial erruptions in 1945–1949, 1960–1963, and 1973–1974. The latest debate on the letters is manifested in a book by Jerzy Smoter of 1967 with counterargument by Mateusz Gliński [see 166]. Presents the essence of each argument and other writing generated by the controversy. The criminological study of the documents (see 164–165) has not ended the debate. Concludes that the controversial letters were prepared through photomontage techniques.

169. Smoter, Jerzy Maria. *Spór o „listy" Chopina do Delfiny Potockiej* [The debate about letters of Chopin to Delfina Potocka]. Biblioteka Chopinowska 11. Kraków: Polskie Wydawnictwo Muzyczne, 1976. 285 p.

Discusses Chopin's relationship with Delfina Potocka. Gives the background of the controversial letters. Evaluates the documents and reviews the arguements for authenticity. Considers the role of Pauline Czernicka. Includes facsimiles of handwriting analysis (see 159), texts of letters, and communications about the letters. Includes a bibliography.

CONTEMPORARY DOCUMENTS

170. Barlow, Jeremy. "Encounters with Chopin: Fanny Erskine's Paris Diary, 1847–8." *Chopin Studies 2*, ed. John Rink and Jim Samson, 245–248. See 300.

Chronicles a two-month period in Paris, December 1847 to January 1848. Provides notes on four meetings with Chopin. Fanny Erskine was close to Schwabe and Jane Stirling.

171. Bauer, Marion. "The Literary Liszt." *Musical Quarterly* 22, no. 3 (July 1936): 295–313.

A short appraisal of the biography *Frédéric Chopin* as one of Liszt's collected literary works. Discusses collaboration on the work with Princess Carolyn von Sayn-Wittenstein.

172. Brunel, Pierre. "Lucrezia Floriani, miroir de la liaison Chopin-Sand." *Revue de musicologie* 75, no. 2 (1989): 147–156.

The author concludes that not too much about the Chopin/Sand relationship should be read into the story. Questions whether Prince Karol is really a portrait of Chopin, as is commonly believed. Challenges comparison point by point.

173. Czerwińska, Teresa. "Dziennik podróży Józefa Kalasantego Jędrzejewicza—nieznany przyczynek do dziejów rodzin Chopinów i Jędrzejewiczów" [Travel journal of J.K. Jędrzejewicz—an unknown note to the history of the Chopin and Jędrzejewicz families]. *Rocznik Chopinowski* 21 (1995): 238–258.

Discusses the journal's background, places it in historical context, and explores the evolution of family relations. An appendix transcribes manuscript fragments of the journal found in different collections.

174. Waters, Edward N. "Chopin by Liszt." *Musical Quarterly* 47, no. 2 (April 1961): 170–194.

A critical look at the romantic and subjective biography by Liszt. Gives the publication history of the book and discusses the role of Princess Carolyn von Sayn-Wittenstein. Considers the Chopin-Liszt friendship, including the complications of sharing the same circle of women and possible jealousy as musicians. The extent of Liszt's authorship is unknown.

A number of publications relate Chopin's life in reproductions of written documents, images, places and other memorabilia. These volumes place the composer in the context of time and place.

175. Czekaj, Kazimierz, ed. *Guide Chopin illustrée.* Warsaw: Chopin Society, 1960. 218 p.

Published for Chopin year 1960 to offer information about commemorative activities. Biography concentrates on early Polish period, providing many illustrations and plates. Lists Chopin's principle concerts. Gives a list of works, selected bibliography, and discography. Large maps of Poland and Warsaw are provided with the volume. Summaries of text in English, Spanish, German, Russian, and Polish.

176. Eigeldinger, Jean-Jacques. "Wspominienia Solange Clesinger o Chopinie." *Rocznik Chopinowski* 12 (1980): 41–54.

177. Eigeldinger, Jean-Jacques. "Frédéric Chopin. Souvenirs inédits par Solange Clésinger." *Revue musical de la Suisse Romande* no. 5 (1978): 224–238.

This reminiscence of Chopin is a document addressed to Sammuel Rocheblue dated 19 January 1896 (Paris, Bibliothèque Nationale, Rés Vcm. ms.23). The *Rocznik Chopinowski* article provides a Polish translation of the text with liberal use of explanatory notes.

178. Fábián, László. *Wenn Chopin ein Tagebuch geführt hätte* . . . Budapest: Druckerei Athenaeum, 1968. 268 p.

Synthetically produces a diary of events in Chopin's life by quoting short excerpts of Chopin's letters and references to Chopin in the letters of other writers.

179. *Frédéric Chopin: Exposition du centenaire.* Paris: Bibliothèque Nationale, 1949. 84 p.

Exhibition catalog covering the life and works of the composer. Documents 234 exhibit items. Includes a name index, reproductions of exhibits.

180.   Kobylańska, Krystyna, ed. *Chopin w kraju: dokumenty i pamiątki*. Kraków: Polskie Wydawnictwo Muzyczne, 1955. 296 p. ML 88.C54 K52

181.   Kobylańska, Krystyna, ed. *Chopin in His Own Land. Documents and Souvenirs*. Trans. Claire Grece-Dąbrowska and Mary Filippi. Kraków: Polskie Wydawnictwo Muzyczne, 1955. 296 p. ML 88.C46 K57

Oversized volume reproduces plates of manuscript pages, illustrations, letters, and newspaper articles concerning Chopin and musical life in Poland during the first half of the nineteenth century. Notes are provided on exhibits, in addition to indices of names and places, a list of archives and private collections, and a bibliography.

182.   Kobylańska, Krystyna. "Nie publikowane dokumenty rodziny Fryderyka Chopina" [Unpublished documents of F. Chopin's family]. *Rocznik Chopinowski* 11 (1978): 75–102.

Provides documentation of the life events of Chopin family from sources such as newspapers and archival documents. Provides a table of documentation.

183.   Mirska, Maria and Władysław Hordyński, eds. *Chopin na obczyźnie: dokumenty i pamiątki* [Chopin abroad: documents and souvenirs]. Kraków: Polskie Wydawnictwo Muzyczne, 1965. 360 p.   ML 88.C46 M57

Oversize volume of reproductions covering Chopin's life after his departure from Poland. Many of the letters are reproduced. Explanatory notes for each item are provided. Includes an indices of names and collections, as well as a bibliography.

184.   Musielak, Henri. "Dokumenty dotyczące spadku po Chopinie" [Documents regarding the bequest after Chopin]. *Ruch Muzyczny* 22, no. 14 (July 2, 1978): 3–7; 22, no. 15 (July 16, 1978): 16–18; 22, no. 16 (July 30, 1978): 14–17.

Traces the disposition of Chopin's property after his death. Provides information about the value of his estate and the role of family and friends in settling his affairs.

185. Musielak, Henri. "Uwagi korektorskie autora" [Corrections of the author]. *Ruch Muzyczny* 24, no. 14 (July 13, 1996): 18–19.

Provides corrections to the 1978 article on Chopin's estate, 184.

186. Wróblewska-Straus, Hanna. "Nowe pamiątki Chopinowskie w zbiorach TiFC" [New Chopin souvenirs in the collections of the Chopin Society]. *Ruch Muzyczny* 22, no. 25 (December 3, 1978): 3–5; 22, no. 26 (December 17, 1998): 16–19.

Discusses the acquisition of documents such as letters, an inventory of Chopin's property, and his passport.

187. Załuski, Iwo, and Pamela Zaluski. *Chopin's Poland.* London: Peter Owen Publishers, 1996. 224 p. ISBN 0720609801 ML 410.C54 Z3189 1996

Concentrates on key scenes related to Chopin's biography and Polish history of the period. Gives background information on nineteenth-century Warsaw and cultural events of the period. Follows Chopin's early travels. Includes a name index.

ICONOGRAPHY

188. Burger, Ernst. *Frederic Chopin. Eine Lebenschronik in Bildern und Dokumenten.* München: Hirmer Verlag, 1990. 358 p. ISBN 3777453706. ML 410. C54 B95 1990

Review: Jeffrey Kallberg, *Notes* 50, no. 3 (March 1994): 963–964.
Photographic reproductions, some in color, follow the biography. Explanatory and source notes provided. Documents presented include photographs, manuscripts, letters, and printed notices. Includes indices of names and works.

189. *Frédéric Chopin, George Sand et leurs amis.* Exposition à la Bibliothèque Polonaise. Paris, 1937.

Exhibit catalog includes an introduction by Léopold Binental. Catalogs 638 items arranged chronologically. Includes letters, musical manuscripts, and iconographic artifacts.

190. Idzikowski, Mieczysław and Bronisław Edward Sydow. *Les portraits de Fryderyk Chopin*. Kraków: Polskie Wydawnictwo Muzyczne, 1953. 137 p.   ML 88.C46 I3

Compiles reproductions of the various artistic representations of Chopin. Includes short commentaries concerning each art work.

191. Idzikowski, Mieczysław and Bronisław Edward Sydow. *Portret Chopina: Antologia ikonograficzna*. Kraków: Polskie Wydawnictwo Muzyczne, 1963. Biblioteka Chopinowska 10. 120 p. ML 88.C46 I27 1963

Compiles photographic reproductions of 128 artistic representations of Chopin. Short commentaries explain the background of each art work. Includes lists of names and archives.

192. Iwaszkiewicz, Jarosław and Adam Kaczkowski. *Żelazowa Wola*. Warszawa: Wydawnictwo Sport i Turystyka, 1965. 65 p.   ML 88.C46 I87 1965

A book of photographs of Chopin's birthplace. The commentary is translated from Polish into English, French, Spanish, German, and Russian.

193. Kański, Józef, and Andrej Zborski. *Chopin i jego ziemia*. [Chopin and the land of his birth]. Warszawa: Wydawnictwo Interpress, 1981. 167 p.   ISBN 8322317735

An album of photographs with an introduction in Polish, Russian, English, French, and German. The captions to the photographic reproductions are also multilingual. Covers the main events in Chopin's life from Żelazowa Wola through Warsaw. Concentrates on artifacts, the importance of his music, and the performance tradition.

194. Sielużycki, Czesław. "Korekty do ikonografii chopinowskiej" [Revisions to Chopin iconography]. *Ruch Muzyczny* 39, no. 3 (5 February 1995): 9–12.

Compares photographs and representations of Chopin with siblings. Items discussed include photographs, daguerreotypes, and the death mask.

CONTEMPORARIES

As revealed in the correspondence, Chopin was acquainted with a number of ninetenth-century musicians and artists. His relationship to George Sand is well known, and there were other famous names in their social circle.

195. Asafvev, B. "Shopen v vospoizvedehii russkikh kompozitorov" [Chopin in the reproduction of Russian composers]. *Sovetskaia Muzyka* 1 (1946): 31–40.

Discusses Chopin's achievements in the context of Russian composers.

196. Chiancone, Adele Cilibrizzi. *Leopardi e Chopin nel clima romantico*. Naples: Edizioni Il Tripode, 1972. 238 p.   PQ 4710.C65

Treats Leopardi and Chopin in parallel. Discusses friends, teachers, and relations to their respective countries. As poet and musician, analyzes their respective role in the development of romanticism. Contains no musical examples, but some quotes from poems. The book depends on Italian secondary sources for information on Chopin. Includes bibliography.

197. Claudon, Francis. "Chopin et la critique romantique: quelque aspects français." *Revue de Musicologie* 75, no. 2 (1989): 157–169.

Analyses writing on Chopin from the perspective of nineteenth-century work exploring the myth of the artist. Writers such as Berlioz, Liszt, Pontmartin, and Legouvé used Chopin's life to express their own sentiments. Only Liszt's biography conveys any of Chopin's Polish character.

198. *The Journal of Eugene Delacroix*. Ed. Hubert Wellington. Trans. Lucy Norton. 3rd ed. London: Phaidon Press, 1995. 504 p. ISBN 0714833592   ND 553.D33 A2

Chopin and other contemporaries are listed in the index. Delacroix gives opinions of music and musicians, as well as other artists of the period.

199.   Sand, George. *Story of My Life: The Autobiography of George Sand,* ed. Thelma Jurgrau. Albany: State University of New York Press, 1991. 1162 p.   ISBN 079140580x   PQ 2412.A2E5 1991

Supports Sand's text with critical and historical introductions. Annotates the text with editorial notes.

200.   Sand, George. *Correspondance.* Ed. Georges Lubin. Paris: Éditions Garnier Frères, 1964–1971. 8 vols.   PQ 2412.A3

Gives and introduction to Sand and the letters, and annotates the letters with explanatory notes. Identifies correspondents. Includes a bibliography and index.

201.   Delaique-Moins, Sylvie. *Chopin chez Georges Sand à Nohant: chronique de sept étés.* Châteauroux, France: Les Amis de Nohant, 1986. 241 p.   ML 410.C54 D45x

Recounts the introduction of Chopin and Sand. Considers the events of each summer that Chopin spent at Nohant: 1839, and 1841–1846. Lists the works that Chopin composed at Nohant, along with the works written by Sand during these periods. Summerizes the Chopin-Sand contact between the summers.

202.   Douël, Martial. "Chopin and Jenny Lind." *Musical Quarterly* 18, no. 3 (July 1932): 423–427.

Reviews Chopin's journey to London in 1848. Lind was a well-regarded Swedish singer performing in London. Chopin was introduced to her by Mrs. Grote when he was invited to her home.

203.   Golos, George S. "Some Slavic Prececessors of Chopin." *Musical Quarterly* 46 (1960): 437–447.

Illustrates with musical examples the similarities and possible influences that Bohemian and Polish composers of the prior generation had on Chopin's musical style.

204.   Kałuża, Zofia. "Chopin i Marcelina Czartoryska" [Chopin and Marcelina Czartoryska]. *Ruch Muzyczny* 18, no. 17 (August 18, 1974): 13–14.

A biography of Czartoryska, emphasizing her lessons with Chopin and the appearance of her name in Chopin's correspondence.

Discusses her playing of Chopin's music and the dedication of compositions to her. Contact between Chopin and Czartoryska during the visits to England are explained.

205. Kirsch, Winfried. "Robert Schumanns Chopin-Bild." *Melos/ Neue Zeitschrift für Musik* 4, no. 3 (1978): 195–200.

Gives a picture of Chopin from the perspective of Schumann. Uses excerpts from Schumann's journals and writings about music.

206. Ladaique, Gabriel. "Mikołaj Chopin w Czerniewice" [N. Chopin in Czerniewicz]. *Ruch Muzyczny* 34, no. 6 (May 6, 1990): 6.

Traces the activites of Chopin's father through the various regions of Poland in the period 1802–1810.

207. Sielużycki, Czesław. "O pochodzeniu matki Chopina" [About the provenance of Chopin's mother]. *Ruch Muzyczny* 33, no. 8 (April 9, 1989): 12–13.

Provides a genealogy, with chart, of the Krzyżanowski family through the eighteenth century.

208. Schumann, Robert. *Music and Musicians: Essays and Criticisms.* Trans. Fanny Raymond Ritter. London: William Reeves, 1880. 540 p.   ML 410.S4 A133 1880

Schumann gives his impressions of newly published music by Chopin through reviews of a number of works, including: Grand Duo for Violin and Piano; Trio, op. 11; Sonata in B flat, Rondo, op. 5; Variations, op. 12; Nocturnes, op. 15; Impromptus, op. 29; Mazurkas, op. 30; Scherzo, op. 31; Tarantella, op. 43.

209. Siwkowska, Janina. *Nokturn czyli rodzina Fryderyka Chopina i Warszawa w latach 1832–1881* [Nocturne, or the family of F. Chopin and Warsaw in the years 1832 to 1881]. Warszawa: Książka i Wiedza, 1986–1996. 3 vols. 498, 462, 475 pp.   ML 410.C54 S63 1986

A well-documented study of the Chopin family. Follows the lives of Chopin, his parents, and siblings. Each volume contains reproductions of portraits, documents, and photographs. Includes a name index.

Chopin is musically related to a number of composers of the nineteenth century. Some are connected because they composed in the same genres.

210.   Smialek, William. *Ignacy Feliks Dobrzyński and Musical Life in Nineteenth-Century Poland.* Studies in the History and Interpretation of Music, 33. Lewiston, N.Y.: Edwin Mellen Press, 1991. 195 p.   ISBN 0889462305   ML 410.D6895S6 1991

Reviews: James Parakilas, *Notes* 50, no. 3 (1994): 962–963; Jerzy Morawski, *Muzyka* 38 (1993): 120–125; Jim Samson, *Music and Letters* 74 (1993): 306–307; Dariusz Pawlas, *Sarmatian Review,* September 1993: 203, 207.

Dobrzyński was a fellow student with Chopin under Elsner in Warsaw. Provides material for a comparison of the early compositional styles of these composers. Also offers extensive information related to Warsaw's musical life in the first few decades of the nineteenth century. Musical examples accompany the discussion of Dobrzyński's works. Includes a list of Dobrzyński's works, a bibliography, and index.

211.   Smidak, Emil F. *Isaak-Ignaz Moscheles: The Life of the Composer and His Encounters with Beethoven, Liszt, Chopin and Mendelssohn.* Brookfield, Vt.: Scolar Press, 1989. 237 p.   ISBN 0859678210   ML 410.M84 S6 1989

Review: Douglass Seaton, *Notes* 48, no. 1 (September 1991): 62–64.

Mentions a few encounters with Chopin. Moscheles met Chopin in 1839. Refers to letters and diary entries regarding Chopin. Reports of the composers performing together.

212.   Tarantová, Marie. "Przyjaciel Chopina Leopold Eustachy Czapek" [Leopold Eustachy Czapek: Friend of Chopin]. *Rocznik Chopinowski* 15 (1983): 29–37.

Provides details about the life of Czapek, a Czech correspondent of Chopin. Reproduces images of this musician and a sample of his music.

213.   Timbrell, Charles. "On the Trail of Liszt, Chopin and Sand: 1834–47." *Piano Quarterly* 34/135 (Fall 1986): 49–56.

Identifies the hotel in Mont Blanc where Liszt, Sand, and Marie d'Agoult stayed in 1836. Gives the historical and biographical background. Describes Sand's estate at Nohant. Compares references in letters and notes with the present museum.

214. Tomaszewski, Mieczysław. *Kompozytorzy polscy o Fryderyku Chopinie* [Polish composers about F. Chopin]. Biblioteka Chopinowska 2. Kraków: Polskie Wydawnictwo Muzyczne, 1980. 183 p. ISBN 8322401396 ML 410.C54 T63

Covers the reception of Chopin and his music from his own time. The anthology of excerpts begin with his teacher Elsner and proceeds through the nineteenth and twentieth centuries.

215. Vuillermoz, Émile. *La vie amoureuse de Chopin.* Paris: Ernest Flammarion, 1927. 184 p. ML 410.C54 V9

Offers a critical assessment of Chopin's relations. Considers Chopin's psyche, as reflected in his music.

216. Vogel, Beniamin. "Zgrowmadzenie organmistrzów i fortepianmistrów w Królestwie Polskim 1815–1918" [The assembly of organ- and pianomakers in the Polish Kingdom 1815–1918]. *Muzyka* 21, no. 4 (1976): 73–76.

Discusses instrument builders in nineteenth-century Warsaw. Gives the names of active builders and quantitative data on instruments in the city.

217. Vogel, Benjamin. "Jeszcze raz o dwóch nieznanych kompozycjach Chopina na eolipantalion" [More about two unknown Chopin compositions for eolipantalion]. *Rocznik Chopinowski* 17 (1985): 123–128.

Discusses the instrument and focuses on the instrument maker Kazimierz Tarczyński and his connection to Chopin.

218. Wernick, Robert. "A Woman Writ Large in Our History and Hearts." *Smithsonian* 27, no. 9 (December 1996): 123–136.

A biographical sketch of author George Sand. Covers her family genealogy, entrance into publishing, work ethic, adoption of male attire, and literary style. Includes photographs of estates and reproductions of art works.

219.   Wodzinski, Antoni. *Les trois romans de Frédéric Chopin.* Paris:
       Calmann-Lévy, 1927. 339 p.   ML 410.C54 W7 1927

       Covers the entire life of Chopin and includes some general cul-
tural information. Concentrates on the composer's relations with Konstancja Gladowska, Maria Wodzińska, and George Sand. Gives a
romanticized story of the relationships.

CHOPIN AS PERFORMER

Relatively little research has illuminated Chopin as a performer. Documentation of private concerts is scanty, leaving much to conjecture.

220.   Eigeldinger, Jean-Jacques. "Les premiers concerts de Chopin à
       Paris (1832–1838): Essai de mise au point." In *Music in Paris in
       the Eighteen-Thirties,* ed. Peter Bloom, 251–297. Stuyvesant,
       N.Y.: Pendragon Press, 1987. 641 p.   ISBN 0918728711   ML
       270.8 P2M76 1987

       Gives reasons for Chopin's limited large concerts in Paris. On
February 26, 1832 Chopin performed the E-minor concerto with string
quartet accompaniment. Sorts actual performances from press an-
nouncements. Five of seventeen performance dates remain uncertain.
Charts the performances in a table with information about press an-
nouncements and reviews, extra programs, the place of the concert, and
sponsor of the event.

221.   Gołos, Jerzy. "Na których organach grał Chopin?" [On which
       organ did Chopin play?] *Ruch Muzyczny* 32, no. 19 (September
       11, 1988): 23.

       Sorts through the Warsaw organs that hold a claim to be the in-
strument played by Chopin.

222.   Hipkins, Edith J. *How Chopin Played: From Contemporary Im-
       pressions Collected from the Diaries and Note-books of the late
       A.J. Hipkins, F.S.A.* London: J.M. Dent and Sons, 1937. 39 p.

       Hipkins was a pioneer in performing Chopin in England, starting
in 1851. Publishes recollections of Chopin in London from 1848 from
notes written in 1899. Hipkins claims that Chopin's "restrained" playing

was not due to physical limitations, but by the pianist-composer's design. The personal reminiscences are augmented with the notes of other contemporaries. Chopin's instruments are discussed in a separate chapter. The appendix provides details of Chopin's funeral and Hiplin's obituary from 1903.

223. Kobylańska, Krystyna. "Improwizacje Fryderyka Chopina" [See next entry]. *Rocznik Chopina* 19 (1987): 69–92.

224. Kobylańska, Krystyna. "Les improvisations de Frédéric Chopin." *Chopin Studies* 3 (1990): 77–103.

Very little is written on Chopin's improvisations. The article reviews references to improvisation by biographers from the nineteenth century. Catalogs references to Chopin's improvisation on known and unknown themes.

225. Poniatowska, Irena. "Improwizacja fortepianowa w okresie romantyzmu" [Piano improvisation in the romantic period]. In *Szkice o kulturze muzycznej XIX wieku* 4, 7–28. Warszawa: Polskie Wydawnictwo Naukowe, 1980. ISBN 8301024186

Reviews the various approaches to improvisation given in early nineteenth-century performance manuals. Studies concert programs from 1830 to 1850 to determine the place of improvisation in concerts. Discusses the practice of performing extemporaneous preludes. Also considers cadenzas. The study incorporates a number of references to Chopin.

226. Szalsza, Piotr. "Koncert, którego nie było" [The concert which did not happen]. *Ruch Muzyczny* 30, no. 6 (March 16, 1986): 17–20.

Reviews documentation of Chopin's Viennese concerts. Proposes that the April 4, 1831 concert was announced, but not held.

227. Pisarenko, Olgierd. "Epoki pianistów i Chopin" [Epochs of pianists and Chopin]. *Ruch Muzyczny* 17, no. 8 (April 16–30, 1973): 17–18.

Places Chopin in a period when pianists were popular as musicians, especially in Paris.

228.   Załuski, Iwo and Pamela Załuski. "Chopin in London." *Musical Times* 133, no. 1791 (May 1992): 226–230.

Summarizes Chopin's trips to London, but concentrates on the trip with Pleyel in 1837. Stresses Chopin's contacts with other Poles during the trip.

229.   Załuski, Iwo and Pamela Załuski. "Frederick Chopin: The Final Concert." *Musical Opinion* 115 (November 1992): 441–442.

Gives the background of Chopin's last London visit. Chopin performed at a charity social event and ball on November 16, 1848 benefiting Polish refugees. He performed the Études op. 25, nos. 1 and 2, as well as several waltzes and mazurkas. Chopin appeared ill and weak throughout the event.

230.   Zieliński, Tadeusz A. "Ilu nauczycieli miał Chopin?" [How many teachers did Chopin have?] *Ruch Muzyczny* 36, no. 6 (March 22, 1992): 7.

Discusses Wilhelm Wacław Würfel as a teacher of Chopin. Based on evidence gleaned from the *Allgemeine musikalische Zeitung*.

CHAPTER 4

Works of the Composer

LIST OF WORKS

The list of Chopin's work is well established and widely available in many reliable references. The following citations relate to the chronology and/or general characteristics of his oeuvre. Also examined are the earliest works of the composer.

231. Harasowski, Adam. "An Overview of Chopin's Piano Music." *Piano Quarterly* 29 (1981): no. 113: 18–32.

   Gives a general overview of the piano music by genre. Isolates Polish elements in the music, particularly Polish dance music and folk sources.

232. Belotti, Gastone. "Le prime composizioni di Chopin." *Rivista italiana di musicologia* 7, no. 2 (1972): 230–291.

   Provides information from newspaper references about Chopin's early works. Writes about the music that is available for study. Uses musical examples.

233. Turło, T. Dalila. "Z zagadnień chronologii piewszych utworów Chopina" [The question of the chronology of Chopin's first works]. *Rocznik Chopinowski* 19 (1987): 145–150.

234. Turło, Teresa Dalila. "Remarques sur la chronologie des première compositions de Chopin." *Chopin Studies* 3 (1990): 199–205.

Reviews previous research on the early works of the composer and identifies mistakes. Refers to both the autograph manuscript tradition and correspondence as sources of information on Chopin's early music. Reviews other nineteenth-century source material.

MANUSCRIPTS AND MANUSCRIPT STUDIES

Study of the manuscripts accounts for many of the recent advances in Chopin research. Catalogs of the manuscript tradition have been grouped with other reference works on the composer and his music. The following citations represent studies of the manuscripts in general and those of specific works.

235.	Kobylańska, Krystyna. "Sur l'histoire des manuscrits de F. Chopin." In *The Book of the First Musicological Congress Devoted to the Works of Frederick Chopin,* ed. Zofia Lissa, 482–487. See 493.

Discusses the enormous task of sorting through the many Chopin manuscripts and copies. Considers separately the history of the manuscripts from the Polish and foreign periods. Traces the manuscripts through their many owners, both institutions and individuals, since the time of the composer.

236.	Hedley, Arthur. "Some Observations on the Autograph Sources of Chopin's Works." In *The Book of the First Musicological Congress Devoted to the Works of Frederick Chopin,* ed. Zofia Lissa, 474–477. See 493.

Copies made by Julian Fontana between 1835 and 1841 have led to confusion about opp. 43, 28, 33, no. 4, and no. 46. Comments on false editions and sets parameters for future manuscript studies.

237.	Jonas, Oswald. "On the Study of Chopin's Manuscripts." *Chopin Jahrbuch* 1 (1956): 142–155.

Elaborates on the difficulties of establishing a definitive Chopin text. Discusses the approach of Brahms for Breitkopf und Härtel. Refers to specific works and discusses variants.

238. Nowik, Wojciech. "Autografy muzyczne jako podstawa badań źródłowych w chopinologii" [Musical autographs as a source of research in Chopin studies]. *Muzyka* 16, no. 2 (1971): 65–84.

Considers autographs as a source of biographical information. Discusses the limitations of traditional sources for a composer's biography. Autograph scores offer the best picture of the composer's creative style. Lists the markings and abbreviations found in Chopin's scores. Compares manuscript sources of the Mazurka, op. 6, no. 4 and the Mazurka, op. 7, no. 4 to published editions.

239. Kallberg, Jeffery. "O klasyfikacji rękopisów Chopina" [About the classification of Chopin's manuscripts]. *Rocznik Chopinowski* 17 (1985): 63–96.

Refines the classification systems of Chopin manuscripts devised by Brown and Kobylańska (see 34 and 32–33). Divides the genesis of Chopin works into the following:

I. Piano version
II. Sketch
III. Autographs for a public
    Performance manuscripts
    Souvenir manuscripts
IV. Copies

Further analyzes the paper evidence of the late manuscripts of Chopin. Presents tables of works written on twelve-stave paper and four-teen-stave paper.

240. Ekier, Jan. "Le problème d'authenticité de six oeuvres de Chopin." In *The Book of the First Musicological Congress Devoted to the Works of Frederick Chopin,* ed. Zofia Lissa, 463–473. See 493.

Initiates discussion of the conditions needed to establish the authenticity of a musical work. Works considered include:

Work	Complete Works
Mazurka in G major	53 and 53bis
Mazurka in D major	54 and 55
Mazurka in C major	57
Contradanse in G-flat major	XVIII
Waltz in E-flat major	IX no. 17
Variations for flute	

241.   Nowik, Wojciech. "Notacja muzyczna Fryderyka Chopina—jej kształt, specyfika i funkcja" [See next entry]. *Rocznik Chopina* 19 (1987): 93–103.

242.   Nowik, Wojciech. "Frédéric Chopin's Musical Notation—Its Form, Specific Features and Function." *Chopin Studies* 3 (1990): 105–129.

Provides some background information on the notational symbols used in Chopin's manuscripts. Catalogs 24 notational comments or signs, indicating their meaning and source. Places these markings in the context of the music, particularly the form and genre.

243.   Wróblewska-Straus, Hanna. "Nieznane rękopisy dzieł Fryderyka Chopina z op. 21, 34, 40 i 49" [See next entry]. *Rocznik Chopinski* 19 (1987): 105–118.

244.   Wróblewska-Straus, Hanna. "Manuscrits inconnus des oeuvres de l'opus 21, 34, 40 et 49 de Frédéric Chopin." *Chopin Studies* 3 (1990): 131–168.

Reproduces photographs of five autographs in the Archiwum Akt Nowych in Warsaw, which are not in the Kobylańska catalog(32–33). Musical works include autographs of the Waltz, op. 34, no. 2 and Polonaises, op. 40, nos. 1 and 2. The collection includes a sketch of the Fantasy in F minor, op. 49, and a piano score to the F minor Concerto, II and III. The presence of these scores in the archive derives from work on the Paderewski edition. The author provides a description and explanation of the provenance of the manuscripts.

245.   Samson, Jim. "An Unknown Chopin Autograph." *Music and Letters* 127, no. 1720 (July 1986): 376–378.

The author worked from a photograph of the autograph to the Polonaise in C minor, op. 40, found in the Paderewski Archive in the Archiwum Akt Nowych in Warsaw. Places the manuscript in context and discusses the musical consequences of revisions.

246.   Adamczyk-Schmid, Bożena. "Warianty tekstu w rękopisach muzycznych Frydryka Chopina z kolekcji Anne-Marie Boutroux de Ferrà w Vademosie" [Textual variants in F. Chopin's music

manuscripts from the Collection of Anne-Marie Boutroux of Vademosa]. *Rocznik Chopinowski* 19 (1987): 135–144.

247. Adamczyk-Schmid, Bożena. "Les variantes du texte de Frédéric Chopin dans les manuscrits musicaux de la collection d'Anne-Marie Boutroux de Ferrà à Valldemosa." *Chopin Studies* 3 (1990): 185–198.

The research studies a collection of Chopin manuscripts held in Majorca. Provides some background information on the muzeum. Discusses eleven autograph manuscripts, and their relation to edited works and other Chopin manuscripts.

248. Nowik, Wojciech. "Fryderyk Chopin's op. 57—from Variantes to Berceuse." In *Chopin Studies,* ed. Jim Samson, 25–40. See 299.

Provides an explanation of Chopin's change of title. The author considers both Chopin's correspondence and the autograph sources. The sketch for op. 57 has the unusual form of a table of four-measure segments with variants. A fair copy shows expansion in accordance with the formal development indicated in the sketch. The later copy reveals changes at the beginning and end, and in the title of the work.

249. Higgins, Thomas. "Etiuda, op. 10, nr 10: Finalne studia tworzenia. Dwoistość dokonania. Rozwiązanie 'humanitarne.'" *Rocznik Chopinowski* 19 (1987): 119–124.

250. Higgins, Thomas. "Progress Toward Completion of the Study op. 10, no. 10: Its Dual Textual Accomplishment and Chopin's Humane Solution." *Chopin Studies* 3 (1990): 169–174.

Discusses different editions of op. 10, no. 10. Reviews the manuscript tradition for expression markings and weighs the merits of different markings. Higgins' perspective on the music is based on his experience as a pianist.

251. Ekier, Jan. "Das Impromptu Cis moll von Frédéric Chopin." *Melos/Neue Zeitschrift für Musik* 4, no. 3 (1978): 201–204.

Traces the piece through the correspondence and the title of fantasy or impromptu. Discusses the manuscripts, both autographs and copies. Creates a typology of the sources for the work.

252. Belotti, Gastone. "Un omaggio di Chopin alla sorella Ludwika: il «Lento con grande espressione»" *Rivista italiana di musicologia* 3, no. 1 (1968): 59–94.

Attempts to reconstruct a lost autograph. Provides a history of nineteenth-century references to the work. The nocturne, dedicated to Chopin's sister, is listed as op. posth; it is notated in the album of Maria Wodzińska. The author creates a schema of manuscripts and editions from the four manuscript sources.

253. Belotti, Gastone. "Nowy mazurek Chopina" [A new Chopin mazurka]. *Rocznik Chopinowski* 17 (1985): 23–62.

Informs us about the manuscript for a G minor Mazurka in the Pierpont Morgan Library. Considers references in Chopin's letters and discusses the music through musical examples. The G minor Mazurka is the first version of the Mazurka in F-sharp minor, op. 57, no. 3.

254. Gajewski, Ferdinand. "Chopin's Dąbrowski Mazurka." *Journal of the American Liszt Society* 32 (1993): 38–41.

Discusses a single leaf of the middle part of the mazurka "Jeszcze Polska nie zginęła," known today as the Polish national anthem. The manuscripts was acquired by the Chopin Society in 1980. The author of the article provides an edition and reconstruction of the work.

255. Kallberg, Jeffrey. "The Problem of Repetition and Return in Chopin's Mazurkas." In *Chopin Studies,* ed. Jim Samson, 1–23. See 299.

Chopin habitually revised works and was often inconsistent. There is a high frequency of changes to repetitions and return patterns in the mazurkas, including bar or phrase repetition, sectional repetition, and sectional return. The author tries to sort out source differences. Chopin differed on when to restate the principle theme or section. In his mature works, minor changes at the end and codas give a more decisive feeling of closure. The printed editions do not express Chopin's alterations. This study sheds light on Chopin's concept of form and closure.

256. Nowik, Wojciech. "Chopinowski konstruktywizm w rękopisach Nocturnu c-moll" [Chopin's constructivism in the manuscripts

of the Nocturne in C minor]. *Rocznik Chopinowski* 14 (1982): 21–32.

Studies the creative process in this musical work through an examination of the manuscripts. Considers the segmentation of the music evidenced in the composer's sketch. Uses charts to discuss the placement of the segments.

257. Belotti, Gastone. "Analiza porównawcze autografu Polonezów op. 26 Chopina" [A comparative analysis of the autographs of Chopin's Polonaise, op. 26]. *Rocznik Chopinowski* 10 (1976–1977): 12–42.

Provides photographic plates of the autograph manuscript. Discusses the publishing and revision processes, continuing into the question of text authenticity. Compares the autograph manuscript with printed editions, covering the music measure by measure.

258. Nowik, Wojciech. "Preludium A moll, op. 28, nr 2 Fryderyka Chopina" [The Prelude in A minor, op. 28, no. 2, of F. Chopin]. *Rocznik Chopinowski* 17 (1985): 97–122.

Reviews the background and scholarship on the Preludes. Discusses the process of creating the A minor prelude, particularly the role of improvisation. Studies the manuscript of the work and analyzes the harmonic structure of the music. Reconsiders dating to 1838–1839.

259. Schachter, Carl. "The Prelude in E minor, op. 28, no. 4: Autograph Sources and Interpretation." In *Chopin Studies 2*, ed. John Rink and Jim Samson, 161–182. See 300.

Describes the notations in two autograph manuscripts that might aid performers and analysts. Provides information on the manuscripts and analyzes the music with Schenkarian techniques. Compares this work with the Mazurka, op. 41, no. 1.

260. Chechlińska, Zofia. "Ze studiów nad źródłami do scherz F. Chopina" [A Study of the Sources of the Scherzos of F. Chopin]. *Annales Chopin* 5 (1960): 82–199.

Reviews autographs, other manuscripts, first editions, and other publications as sources for Chopin scherzos. Compares different versions of the scherzos as transmitted in the sources. Considers some editions to have romantic characteristics, whereas others have classical traits. Includes a summary in French.

261.   Gajewski, Ferdinand, ed. *The Work Sheets to Chopin's Violoncello Sonata: A Facsimile.* New York: Garland, 1988. 110 p. ISBN 0824026608   ML 96.4 C45

Review: Jeffrey Kallberg, *Notes* 46 (March 1990): 801–803.

The study begins with an introductory essay on the cello sonata, including extensive background information on the André manuscript collection. The facsimile edition derives from photographs provided to Ludwik Bronarski before the break-up of the collection, supplemented with photographs from other sources. The manuscripts and edition contain parts of other works. Many of the manuscript pages are presently housed in the collections of the Chopin Society in Warsaw.

262.   Kobylańska, Krystyna. "Autograf roboczy partytury Wariacji B dur, op. 2, Fryderyka Chopina" [The Autograph of the Variations in B-flat major, op. 2, of F. Chopin]. *Ruch Muzyczny* 23, no. 23 (November 18, 1979): 14–15.

Provides notes from an examination of the manuscript, which is owned by the Lehman Foundation. The author illuminates misreadings of the markings on the manuscript.

263.   Chainaye, Suzanne and Denise. "Un valse inédite de Frédéric Chopin." *Revue de musique* no. 226 (1955): 211–232.

Provides facsimiles of two manuscripts and an edition of the music. The commentary discusses the contributions of English musicologists to Chopin studies. The Waltz in A minor is generally unknown, but was found in Paris libraries.

264.   Belotti, Gastone. "Un nuovo valzer di Chopin?" *Nuova rivista musicale italiana* 12, no. 4 (1978): 521–541.

The article concerns the Waltz in F-sharp minor published in New York in 1932. Discusses the background of the music, sources, and authenticity. Continues with an analysis of the music itself.

265. Brooks, Muriel. "Chopin/Janis." *American Music Teacher* 28, no. 5 (1979): 6–8.

Tells the story of Byron Janis' discovery of manuscripts of the Waltz in G-flat major, op. 70, and the Waltz in E-flat major, op. 18. Reflects on the differences in versions of the manuscripts.

266. Parker, Carol Mont. "Chopin Waltz Manuscripts." *Clavier* 18, no. 7 (1979): 8–13.

Summarizes the study *Chopin/Janis: The Most Dramatic Musical Discovery of the Age.* Explains the background of the manuscripts. Provides some analysis of the music and comparison of sources.

PUBLICATIONS HISTORY

The publication of Chopin's compositions is complicated by his simultaneous business negotiations with publishing firms in different countries and his revision of works after the original manuscript stage. Jeffrey Kallberg has led the research efforts to understand the publication process.

267. Kallberg, Jeffrey. "Chopin in the Marketplace: Aspects of the International Music Publishing Industry in the First Half of the Nineteenth Century." *Notes* 39, no. 3 (1983): 535–569; *Notes* 39, no. 4 (1983): 795–824.

Probes issues of the publication of Chopin's music and how the composer dealt with publishers in France, England, and the German-speaking states. Sorts out the multiple editions of Chopin's works and the variants among them. Addresses copyright registration, sources used to prepare each edition, and control over the published text. The author discusses how Chopin coordinated business internationally to gain the maximum benefit. Research relies on correspondence and archival information. Includes tables of documentation data.

268. Kallberg, Jeffrey. "Compatibility in Chopin's Multipartite Publications." *Journal of Musicology* 2, no. 4 (1983): 391–417.

The article concerns the unity of pieces published together as a set. Reviews the limited documentation of Chopin's intentions. Investigates tonal relations among works and the importance of the coda.

Concludes that Chopin performed works individually and made works in the sets compatible.

269.   Turło, Teresa Dalila. "Problemy identyfikacji i chronologii pier-
        wszych wydań Chopina" [Problems of identification and
        chronology of Chopin's first publications]. *Rocznik Chopinowski*
        14 (1982): 33–53.

Chopin's music was first published by the firms of Cybulski and Brzezina in Warsaw, and then T. Haslinger in Vienna. After Chopin's arrival in Paris, other publishers became interested in his music. Discusses problems of identifying first editions. Offers a chronology in chart form covering the period 1825–1848.

270.   Einstein, Alfred. "Opus 1." *Musical Quarterly* 20, no. 4 (October
        1934): 367–383.

A history of first works presented to the public by various composers. Chopin's opus 1 merited the public note of Schumann.

271.   Brown, Maurice J.E. "The Chronology of Chopin's Preludes."
        Musical Times No. 1374 (August 1957): 423–424.

Discusses the reservation of op. 28 in the publishing sequence. The author connects the composition to the trip to Majorca. Tentatively dates the creation of the various preludes between 1836 and 1839.

272.   Brown, Maurice J.E. "The Posthumous Publication of Chopin's
        Songs." *Musical Quarterly* 42, no. 1 (January 1956): 51–65.

Describes the nineteen songs and texts of the five poets selected by the composer. Some of the songs were initially written in albums. Considers the role of Julian Fontana in publishing the songs and the notes in various letters about the collection and publication of the works. Discusses early editions, beginning with *16 Polnische Lieder,* op. 74, the first published version.

EDITIONS

Chopin's works have been edited for publication in several series since the nineteenth century. Prominent among the collected works editions are the Paderewski edition, the Henle Verlag Urtext edition, and the Polish National Edition.

273.   F.F. *Chopin: Dzieła wszystkie* [Complete works]. Ed. Ignacy J. Paderewski, Ludwik Bronarski, and Józef Turczyński. Warsaw and Kraków: Polskie Wydawnictwo Muzyczne, 1949–1961. M3 C584

274.   *Wydanie Narodowe Dzieł Fryderyka Chopina* [National Edition of the Works of F. Chopin]. Ed. Jan Ekier. Kraków: Polskie Wydawnictwo Muzyczne, 1967–.

275.   Chopin, Frédéric. *Works*. Ed. Ewald Zimmermann. München: G. Henle Verlag, 1963–.   M22 C545

276.   Idzikowski, Mieczysław. "Dzieła Chopina pod redakcją Paderewskiego" [The works of Chopin edited by Paderewski]. *Ruch Muzyczny* 12, no. 6 (March 15–31, 1968): 14–15.

Gives the background of the Paderewski edition of Chopin's works. Explains the assistance of Ludwik Bronarski and Józef Turczyński.

277.   Chechlińska, Zofia. "O Wydawaniu Narodowym Dzieł Chopina" [About the national edition of Chopin's works]. *Rocznik Chopinowski* 15 (1983): 15–28.

Discusses the need, goals, methodology, and status of the source critical edition of Chopin's works edited by Jan Ekier.

278.   Grabowski, Krzysztof. "Francuskie oryginalne wydania dzieł Fryderyka Chopina" [Original French publications of Chopin's works]. *Rocznik Chopinowski* 21 (1995): 115–155.

Provides some background and history of the publication of Chopin works by French publishers. Gives information not available in Kallberg's study (267), nor Chomiński-Turło, *Katalog dzieł F. Chopina* (35). Provides a table of works published with dates. The article covers each publisher and work.

279.   Brown, Maurice J.E. "First Editions of Chopin in Periodicals and Serial Publications." *Annales Chopin* 5 (1960): 7–12.

Discusses periodicals from different countries that include Chopin works. Polish publications include the largest number of first editions. Covers editions published in the nineteenth and twentieth centuries.

280.   Kallberg, Jeffrey. "Czy warianty są problemem? 'Intencje kom-
       pozytorskie w edytorstwie dzieł Chopina" [See next entry].
       Rocznik Chopinowski 19 (1987): 199–210.

281.   Kallberg, Jeffrey. "Are Variants a Problem? Composer's Inten-
       tions in Editing Chopin." *Chopin Studies* 3 (1990): 257–267.

       Studies the consequences of variants in editing Chopin's music.
       Review of different manuscripts leads to a better of understanding of the
       composer's intentions. Compares different versions of specific pieces
       through musical examples. Selects for study the Nocturne in B major, op.
       62, no. 1; Waltz in D-flat major, op. 64, no. 1; and Étude in E major, op.
       10, no. 3.

282.   Jonas, Oswald. "Ein textkritisches Problem in der Ballade op. 38
       von Frédéric Chopin." *Acta musicologica* 35, no. 2–3 (1963):
       155–158.

       Reviews Heinrich Schenker's notes on the Johannes Brahms-
       Ernst Rudorff correspondence concerning different editions of Chopin's
       music. Makes reference to specific measures of problematic passages.
       Schenker's opinion of possible editorial solutions is taken from his
       letters.

283.   Zimmermann, Ewald. "Probleme der Chopin-Edition." *Musik-
       forschung* 14 (1961): 155–165.

       A reflection on the Henle edition by the editor. Reviews the prob-
       lems of editing Chopin and the various sources of the études. Prints
       detailed notes to revise the published editions of the Études, opp. 10
       and 25.

ANALYTICAL WRITING

It is difficult to separate analytical writing from studies in compositional
style. Within each of these categories, however, references can be
grouped according to the same plan. Following research that broadly addresses Chopin's music, studies are sorted by musical element or genre.
It is of interest to note that some works have attracted much attention as
different musical explanations and interpretations are tested. The Preludes, op. 28, in this regard, have received close scrutiny. Also evident

are changing views of Chopin's problematic musical structures. As research progresses, attention has turned from sonata elements in the ballades to narrative processes. Prominent in recent literature is the application of Schenkarian reductive techniques. As Heinrich Schenker applied his theories to the music of Chopin, analysts have adapted graphing procedures in various ways to explain Chopin's complex tonal and structural schemes. The presence of folk influences in the music also has a place in analytical writing. This, of course, is important to consideration of Chopin as Polish nationalist.

284.   Barbedette, H[ippolyte]. *F. Chopin: Essai de critique musicale.* 2nd ed. Paris: Heugel et Cie., 1869. 78 p.   ML 410.C54B17

A series of essays on Chopin's biography and different genres of his music. Discusses influences and national chararacter in the music. No musical examples are incorporated into the text.

285.   Chomiński, Józef. "Mistrzostwo kompozytorskie Chopina" [The Composer's Mastery of Chopin]. *Rocznik Chopinowski* 1 (1956): 171–226.

The article begins by questioning what it means to be a musical master. Reviews the literature on the style and compositional techniques of Chopin, and the composer's contribution to the development of piano texture. Considers Chopin as a romantic master and representative of Polish nationalism in music.

286.   Davison, J.W. *Frederic Chopin: Critical and Appreciative Essay.* London: Wm. Reeves, n.d. 29 p.

Places the music in an historical context while commenting on the biography. The author takes the position that "the art of Chopin must be either accepted or rejected; it will not stand the test of criticism." (p. 20). Gives rather general comments about the music.

287.   Eigeldinger, Jean-Jacques. "Placing Chopin: Reflections on a Compositional Aesthetic." In *Chopin Studies 2*, ed. John Rink and Jim Samson, 102–139. See 300.

Chopin adhered to the artistic grounding of his training in Poland. The author ties events in Chopin's later life to early influences. Chopin was not interested in "modern" composers of his day, but in the musical past. Presents specific examples of references to the past. Reviews evidence of Chopin's veneration for Bach and Mozart. Compares Chopin's views to those of Debussy and relates his interest in Beethoven's Sonata, op. 26.

288.   Federhofer, Hellmut. "Dzieła Chopina jako przykłady w podręcznikach z zkresu teorii muzyki" [The works of Chopin as examples in music theory textbooks]. *Rocznik Chopinowski* 19 (1987): 157–162.

Notes examples taken from Chopin works for books on music beginning with the writing of François Joseph Fétis and Ignaz Mocheles. Chopin composed three études specifically for the *Méthode de Méthodes de Piano*. Other works are cited by nineteenth-century writers, including musical examples in French and German theory handbooks. Chopin's harmonic devises are particularly noted. Chopin's music was studied by Heinrich Schenker.

289.   Jachimecki, Zdislas. *Frédéric Chopin et son oeuvre*. Paris: Librarie Delagrave, 1930. 244 p.   ML 410.C54 J143

Begins with a short biographical essay. Discusses the music by genre. Uses only a few musical examples. Concludes with an essay on Chopin's style.

290.   Jonson, G.C. Ashton. *A Handbook to Chopin's Works*. Boston: Longwood Press, 1978. 287 p.   ISBN 0893410780   ML 410.C54J8 1978 (Reprint; originally published 1912.)

Gives general comments on each genre of composition. More attention is then given to each piece in the form of program notes for pianists and listeners. Each annotation is a brief account of the piece with distinguishing features of the music. Contains a short biography of Chopin, an annotated bibliography, and table of works.

291.   Kelley, Edgar Stillman. *Chopin the Composer: His Structural Art and Its Influence on Contemporary Music*. New York: G. Schirmer, 1913. 190 p.   ML 410.C54 K4 1913

Talks about Chopin's works, grouping them by compositional device or form. A chapter considers national elements in Chopin's music.

Results in a theoretical overview of the music. Includes a name index and list of compositions cited.

292. Lissa, Zofia. *Studia nad twóczością Fryderyka Chopina* [Studies on the Creativity of F. Chopin]. Biblioteka Chopinowska, 12. Kraków: Polskie Wydawnictwo Muzyczne, 1970. 510 p. ML 410.C54 L663

Contains studies on the national style in Chopin's music, the Fantasy in F minor, op. 49, Chopin's style related to Beethoven, Scriabin, and Reger, and Chopin's harmony as a precurser of twentieth-century techniques. The essays are reprints of earlier articles; original publication information is noted. Includes indices of Chopin's works, as well as the names and works of other composers.

293. Lissa, Zofia. *F.F. Chopin*. Warszawa: Uniwersytet Warszawski, 1960. 333 p. ML 410.C54 F2

A compilation of essays on Chopin by prominent Polish scholars. Studies works in Chopin's genres before the composer, theoretical aspects of his music, and the performance tradition. Summaries are provided in English, French, and Russian.

294. Mazel, Lew. *Studia chopinowskie* [Chopin Studies]. Trans. Jerzy Popiel. Biblioteka Chopinowska 8. Kraków: Polskie Wydawnictwo Muzyczne, 1965. 337 p. ML 410.C54 M44

Includes an extended analytical study of the Fantasie in F minor, supported with numerous musical examples. The studies also address Chopin's melodies and free-form compositions. The list of publications includes many printed in Russian. Provides indexes of names and works cited.

295. Rehberg, Walter and Paula Rehberg. *Frédéric Chopin: Sein Leben und sein Werk*. Zürich: Artemis Verlag, 1949. 565 p. ML 410.C54 R37

After presenting the facts of Chopin's life, the book discusses individual works grouped by genre. Gives historical background to the works. Includes a year-by-year chronology, list of works, name index, subject index, and bibliography.

296.   Rosen, Charles. "Chopin: Counterpoint and the Narrative Forms."
       In *The Romantic Generation,* 279–471. Cambridge: Harvard Uni-
       versity Press, 1995. 723 p.   ISBN 0674779339   ML 196.R67
       1995

Discusses problems in specific Chopin works through the musical evidence. Points out that Chopin was a master of counterpoint and
very familiar with Johann Sebastian Bach's *Well-Tempered Clavier.*
Generalizes about Chopin and nineteenth-century music from specific
examples. Covers all genres, but concentrates on the ballades, études, the
Sonata in B-flat minor, and the Polonaise in F-sharp minor, op. 44.

297.   Samson, Jim. *The Music of Chopin.* Oxford: Clarendon Press,
       1985. 243 p.   ISBN 0198164025   ML 410.C54 S188 1985

Begins with a biographical sketch that increases our understanding of Chopin's formative Polish period and the social life he experi-
enced in Paris. The music is covered chronologically. The author has a
deep understanding of the music, which includes the cultural context,
theories of analysis and reception, aesthetics, and applicable history. Includes a bibliography, list of works, and index.

298.   Samson, Jim, ed. *The Cambridge Companion to Chopin.* Cam-
       bridge: Cambridge University Press, 1992. 341 p.   ISBN
       0521404908   ML 410.C54 C2 1992

Review: Kofi Agawu, *Notes* 51, no. 1 (September 1994): 135–138.
Begins with a biographical introduction considering Chopin's reception as a salon composer, romantic composer, and Slavonic composer. Supports the study with a chronology of events of Chopin's life.
Distinguishes the myths from reality. Essays by a number of authors are
grouped into the categories of style development, individual genres, and
reception studies. Gives a list of works, bibliographic notes, and an index.

299.   Samson, Jim, ed. *Chopin Studies.* Cambridge: Cambridge Univer-
       sity Press, 1988. 258 p.   ISBN 0521303656.   ML 410.C54 C48

Review: Douglass Seaton, *Notes* 48, no. 1 (September 1991):
62–64.
Essays cover the composer's intentions derived from autograph
manuscripts, aspects of Chopin's musical language, and studies of individual works—Preludes, op. 28; Barcarolle; and Fantasy, op. 49.

300. Rink, John and Jim Samson, eds. *Chopin Studies 2*. Cambridge: Cambridge University Press, 1994. ISBN 0521416477 ML 410.C54C48

Essays consider reception history, aesthetics, and criticism, and performance studies.

301. Kallberg, Jeffrey. *Chopin at the Boundaries: Sex, History, and Musical Genre*. Cambridge, Mass.: Harvard University Press, 1996. 301 p. ISBN 0674127900 ML 410.C54K16

A collection and reconsideration of previously published essays by the author. Synthesizes much of the recent scholarship on Chopin to present him in a new light. Extensive notes document the essays. Includes an index.

Form

302. Dalila, Teresa Turło. "Dziedzictwo formy artystycznej Chopina" [The Heritage of the Artistic Forms of Chopin]. *Rocznik Chopinowski* 8 (1969): 7–43.

Presents the historiography of analyses and interpretations of the form of Chopin's music. Discusses the sources for the music, the role of editors, and differing interpretations from the contrasting viewpoints of classicism and romanticism. Provides a summary of the article in French.

303. DeLong, Kenneth. "Roads Taken and Retaken: Foreground Ambiguity in Chopin's Prelude in A-flat, op. 28, no. 17." *Canadian University Music Review* 11, no. 1 (1991): 34–49.

Discusses moments of ambiguity in musical works, drawing on examples in Beethoven and Schubert. Probes the structural implications of two modulating episodes in Chopin's Prelude no. 17.

304. Griffel, L. Michael. "The Sonata Design in Chopin's Ballades." *Current Musicology* 36 (1983): 125–136.

Begins with a background on the sonata in the nineteenth century. Discusses how Chopin adjusted the form to meet the requirements of his romantic nature. Discusses the sonata features of each ballade. Concludes that sonata designs became increasingly remote as Chopin's career progressed.

305.   Hofstadter, Douglas R. "Metamagical Themas: The Music of
        Frédéric Chopin: Startling Aural Patterns that Also Startle the
        Eye." *Scientific American* 246, no. 4 (April 1982): 16–28.

306.   Hofstadter, Douglas R. *Metamagical Themas: Questing for the
        Essence of Mind and Pattern.* New York: Basic Books, 1985. 852
        p.   ISBN 0553342797   Q 335.H63 1986

Analyzes piano textures using a computer to discern patterns evident to the ear, but not immediately visual. Attempts to understand "pat-
terned complexity" of the Études op. 10 and op. 25. Refers to the visual
patterns of Chopin manuscripts. The article was reprinted with a post-
scriptum in 1985.

307.   Kaiser, Joachim. "Chopin und die Sonate." In *Musik-Konzepte 45
        Fryderyk Chopin,* ed. Heinz-Klaus Metzger and Rainer Riehn,
        3–16. München: Text + Kritik, 1985.   ISBN 3883771988   ML
        410.C54 F78 1985

Review: Detlef Gojowy, *Neue Zeitschrift für Musik* 147, no. 9
(September 1986): 80–81.
Considers all of Chopin's works based on the sonata principle:
concertos, rondos, sonatas, and so forth. The article contains many musical examples. The author takes the position that Chopin had difficulty
reconciling the Polish character of his music with the requirements of
sonata form.

308.   Klein, Rudolf. "Chopins Sonatentechnik." *Österreichische
        Musikzeitschrift* 22, no. 7 (1967): 389–399.

Approaches the Chopin sonatas as a problem in content versus
form. Reviews each sonata composition. Discusses musical examples of
motivic relations.

309.   Protopopow, Włodzimierz. "Forma cyklu sonatowego w ut-
        worach F. Chopina" [The form of the sonata cycle in the works of
        F. Chopin]. In *Polsko-rosyjskie miscellanea muzyczne,* ed. Zofia
        Lissa, 126–140. Kraków: Polskie Wydawnictwo Muzyczne,
        1967. 469 p.

Considers the seven Chopin works cast in sonata form. Discusses
the general structure and tonal plans. Considers the different movements.

310. Protopopov, Vladimir. "A New Treatment of Classical Music Forms in Chopin's Compositions." *Chopin Studies* 3 (1990): 21–26.

Considers sonata form, especially the recapitulation sections, ternary form as found in the scherzos, and variation form. Chopin is considered through the views on form of Alexander Stasov.

Harmony

311. Benedetto, Daniela. "La funzione timbrica dell'armonia nelle composizioni di Fryderyk Chopin." *Nuova rivista musicale italiana* 18, no. 2 (1984): 217–252.

Finds the roots of Chopin technique in earlier composers. Reviews the literature on analysis of the sound or timbre in Chopin's compositions. Takes short examples from a variety of works to investigate different sound combinations in the piano texture. Compares Chopin's approach to other nineteenth-century composers.

312. Chomiński, Józef M. "Harmonika a faktura fortepianowa Chopina" [The harmony and piano texture of Chopin]. *Muzyka* 4, no. 4 (1959): 3–25.

Reviews the analysis of Chopin's harmony by several writers. Formulates an additional view of Chopin's harmony and texture. Supports concepts with references to Chopin works.

313. Cone, Edward T. "Ambiguity and Reinterpretation in Chopin." In *Chopin Studies 2*, ed. John Rink and Jim Samson, 140–160. See 300.

Overfamiliarity with atypical harmonic patterns causes us to not appreciate the ambiguity in many Chopin passages. The author reanalyzes passages as the composer intended them to be heard. Considers short passages that play with alternative reactions to harmonic or polyphonic detail, rhythmic dislocation, and additions or omissions in form.

314. Gołąb, Maciej. "Das Problem der Haupttonart in den Werken von Chopin." *Chopin Studies* 5 (1995): 235–244.

Addresses the issue of tonal instability in Chopin's music. Considers the context of nineteenth-century chromatic harmony. Relates tonality with genre, discussing various examples.

315. Kinderman, William. "Directional Tonality in Chopin." In *Chopin Studies,* ed. Jim Samson, 59–75. See 299.

Studies three works that begin in a secondary tonality: the Scherzo, no. 2, op. 31; the Fantasy, op. 49; the Ballade no. 2, op. 38. In these works, tonic keys are treated not as a initial point of orientation, but as the goal of a directional process.

316. Narmour, Eugene. "Melodic Structuring of Harmonic Dissonance: A Method for Analysing Chopin's Contribution to the Development of Harmony." In *Chopin Studies,* ed. Jim Samson, 77–114. See 299.

Shows that certain melodic patterns in Chopin's music generate a large pool of dissonant sonorities that come to function structurally. This large vocabulary of sonorities forms an integral part of Chopin's harmonic language. Explores the relationship between melodic structures and the treatment of dissonance. Examines four types of melodic structure: process, reversal, processive reversal, and registral return.

Melody

317. Colombati, Claudia. "Chopin a Bellini" [Chopin and Bellini]. *Ruch Muzyczny* 19, no. 21 (November 12, 1975): 3–5.

Discusses Chopin's interest in Italian opera and explores the melodic similarities that his music shares with that of Bellini. The study was taken from a dissertation.

318. Federhofer, Hellmut. "Die Diminution in den Klavierwerken von Chopin und Liszt." In *Report of the Second International Musicological Conference, Budapest 1961. Studia musicologica* 5 (1963): 49–57.

Discusses ornaments, cadence types, and arpeggios. Contrasts the styles of Chopin and Liszt. Cites numerous works, but only prints one musical example.

319. Pattison, F.L.M. "A Folk-Tune Associated with Chopin and Liszt." *Journal of the American Liszt Society* 20 (1986): 38–41.

The folk tune is from an autograph manuscript noted by Eigeldinger in the *Schweizerische Musikzeitung* (1975). The same melody was also employed by Liszt. Considers the dating of the respective works.

320. Sobieska, Jadwiga. "Problem cytatu u Chopina" [The problem of quotation in Chopin]. *Muzyka* 4, no. 4 (1959): 74–100.

Identifies Chopin's quotations from Polish folk music. Many musical examples discuss folk references. Addresses rhythms as well as melodies.

Rhythm and Meter

321. Hlawiczka, Karol. "Reihende polymetrische Erscheinungen in Chopins Musik." *Annales Chopin* 3 (1958): 68–99.

Investigates rhythmic groupings of three against two and other rhythmic complexities of Chopin's music. Considers these patterns, and such rhythmic devices as hemiola and syncopation, to be examples of polymeter. Extensive use of musical examples.

322. Prost, Christine. "Modernité de F. Chopin: La dynamique et la timbre comme éléments constitutifs de la forme." *Analyse musicale* 8 (June 1987): 27–30.

Analyzes the Prelude in B-flat minor, considering the harmonic and dynamic rhythm. Examines the Étude in F minor for melody and timbre. Relates these elements of music to form.

323. Rothstein, William. "Phrase Rhythm in Chopin's Nocturnes and Mazurkas." *Chopin Studies,* ed. Jim Samson, 115–141. See 299.

Reviews the history of the piano character piece with regard to the "rhythm problem," the issue of the four-bar phrase, and the enhancement of melodic continuity. Analyzes hypometer. Schenkarian voice-leading graphs isolate Chopin's use of lead-ins and connective third progressions to avoid a stark division between successive melodic segments. Works studied include: Nocturnes, op. 9, no. 2; op. 32, no. 1; op. 48, no. 2; op. 62, nos. 1 and 2; and Mazurkas, op. 17, no. 3; op. 59, no. 1.

Tempo

324.   Higgins, Thomas. "Tempo i character utworów Chopina"
       [Tempo and character of Chopin's works]. *Rocznik Chopinowska*
       18 (1989): 93–105.

Studies the metronome markings in autograph manuscripts of
works from 1827 to 1836. Provides musical examples to compare the
markings with the character of the music. Includes a table of metronome
indications.

Texture

325.   Chechlińska, Zofia. "The Nocturnes and Studies: Selected Prob-
       lems of Piano Texture." In *Chopin Studies,* ed. Jim Samson,
       143–165. See 299.

Discusses texture as related to piano fabric. The études are a
compendium of figuration in many differing varieties. The nocturnes dis-
play cantilena melodic lines with harmonic accompaniment.

Timbre and Instrumentation

326.   Michniewicz, Grażyna. "Wiolonczela w twórczości Fryderyka
       Chopina" [The violoncello in the creations of F. Chopin].
       Rocznik Chopinowski 16 (1984): 25–65.

Compares the sources of works with violoncello. Reviews the
critical comments of other writers and places the works in the context of
Chopin's biography. Discusses the technical aspects of the violoncello
parts through musical examples. Considers the use of the violoncello in
chamber music and relates Chopin's approach to that of other Polish
composers of chamber music.

327.   Zimmermann, Ewald. "Chopin i jego orkiestra" [Chopin and his
       orchestra]. *Rocznik Chopinowski* 19 (1987): 125–133.

Reopens the issue of Chopin's orchestration of the concertos,
particularly the question of whether he was assisted by Ignacy Feliks Dobrzyński. Discusses the orchestra of the period. Traces the publication

history of the concertos and changes in the orchestration to meet the performance situation.

328. Zimmermann, Ewald. "Chopin und sein Orchester: Fragen zur Quellenlage und zur Authentizität der Instrumentation in den Klavierkonzerten." *Chopin Studies* 3 (1990): 175–183.

Considers all the instrumental writing of the composer and especially the string quartet reductions of accompaniments to the concertos. Discusses the orchestral practice of the period and different published versions of the concertos. Gives in-depth study to the manuscripts.

Ballades

329. Berger, Karol. "Chopin's Ballade, op. 23, and the Revolution of the Intellectuals." In *Chopin Studies 2*, ed. John Rink and Jim Samson, 72–83.

Explains the formal logic of the Ballade, op. 23. Compares the musical form with the historical consciousness of the Polish emigré community in nineteenth-century Paris. Reviews intellectual history of nineteenth-century revolutions and places Chopin in the context of the prominent ideologies and related activities. Ideas converge with consideration of the ballade as musical narrative.

330. Bogdańska, Anna. "Technika wariacyna i praca tematyczna w balladach Chopina" [Variation technique and thematic work in the ballades of Chopin]. *Rocznik Chopinowska* 18 (1989): 63–91.

Reviews the literature on variation technique in Chopin. Discusses introduction sections and their signifiance in the thematic working of the music. Treats the four ballads comparatively. Synthesizes development techniques through musical examples.

331. Eibner, Franz. "Über die Form der Ballade, op. 23, von Fr. Chopin." *Annales Chopin* 3 (1958): 107–112.

Provides a table delineating the form of the work. References are made to the analytical approach of Schenker.

332.   Gut, Serge. "Interferences entre le langage et la structure dans la
        Ballade en sol mineur, opus 23, de Chopin." *Chopin Studies* 5
        (1995): 64–72.

Reviews the reason for the ballade title and other analyses of the
G-minor ballade. Examines the content, style, and tonal plan of the work.
Presents a chart of the ballade's structure.

333.   Rink, John. "Ballady Chopina i dialektyka metod analitycznych:
        Analiza z perspektywy historycznej" [Chopin's ballades and di-
        alectical analytical methods: Analysis from historical perspec-
        tives]. *Rocznik Chopinowski* 21 (1995): 45–66.

Reviews studies on the ballades, both historical and theoretical.
Sorts through the different approaches to provide a meta analysis. Reproduces key musical examples and graphs.

334.   Samson, Jim. Chopin: *The Four Ballades*. Cambridge Music Hand-
        books. Cambridge: Cambridge University Press, 1992. 104 p.
        ISBN 0521384613   ML 410.C47 P6 1992

Review: Wojciech Nowik, *Rocznik Chopinowski* 21 (1989):
345–350; Agnieszka Chwiłek and Paweł Gancarczyk, *Muzyka* 39, no. 2
(1994): 112–115.
Examines the four ballades from historical and analytical perspectives. Covers the background from 1820s Warsaw to Paris. Discusses the genesis, reception, and form of each of the works. Further
considers the ballade as a genre.

335.   Samson, Jim. "The Second Ballade—Historical and Analytical
        Perspectives." *Chopin Studies* 5 (1995): 73–81.

Concentrates on the function of a two-key scheme, separating the
style of the work from the structure. Reviews a variety of theories that
may be applied to the work. Finds an historical context in postclassical
popular concert music and other early romantic music.

336.   Tarasti, Eero. "A Narrative Grammar of Chopin's G minor Bal-
        lade." *Chopin Studies* 5 (1995): 38–63.

Analyzes the work by applying narrative and semiotic method-
ologies. Applies the semiotic theory of Algirdes Julien Greimas to the G
minor Ballade. Provides charts with musical examples.

Barcarolle

337.   Rink, John. "The *Barcarolle*: *Auskomponierung* and apotheosis." *Chopin Studies*, pp. 195–219. See 299.

Considers the work as a structural synthesis, with interest provided by the variety of methods Chopin uses to fill in the tonal framework. The author adopts a Schenkarian approach, using voice-leading graphs. Separately discusses the background, middle ground, foreground, phrase structure, and the effect of pedaling.

338.   Salmen, Walter. "Die Barkarole vor Chopin: Herkunft und Semantik eines musikalischen Genres." *Chopin Studies* 5 (1995): 198–209.

Gives some background on the barcarolle as a genre. Places the Chopin work in the context of music by other nineteenth-century composers. Prints musical examples of melodic types and accompaniment figures.

Concertos

339.   Rink, John. *Chopin: The Piano Concertos*. Cambridge: Cambridge University Press, 1997. 139 p.   ISBN 0521441099   ML 410.C54 RR54 1997

Prepares the background by discussing the early nineteenth-century concerto and Chopin's early music. Reviews interpretive essays on concertos and gives analytical notes on each movement. Considers the Allegro de concert, op. 46, as the third Chopin concerto. Includes lists of performance by Chopin, editions, and a discography.

Études

340.   Handman, Dorel. "Chopin: Influence on Two Liszt Etudes." *Musical America* 49, no. 3 (February 1949): 28, 164.

Begins by comparing two F minor works: Chopin's op. 10, no. 9, and Liszt's *Étude d'execution transcendante* no. 10. Also compares Chopin's Étude op. 25, no. 2, with Liszt's *Leggierezza*. Includes several short musical examples.

341.   Smith, Charles J. "(Supra-) Durational Patterns in Chopin's Rev-
        olutionary Etude." *In Theory Only* 2, no. 5 (August 1976): 3–12.

Uses extensive musical examples to isolate rhythmic patterns and
proportions in this analysis of Étude, op. 10, no. 12.

342.   Tomaszewski, Mieczysław. "Ze badań nad rezonansem muzyki
        Chopina: Etiuda a moll, op. 25, nr. 11 w świetle jej słownych in-
        terpretacji" [From research on the resonance of Chopin's music.
        The Étude in A minor, op. 25, no. 11, in light of its interpretation
        vocabulary]. *Rocznik Chopinowski* 21 (1995): 17–44.

Examines the descriptive words used to analyze this work
throughout the literature on Chopin and his music. Offers a model that
takes a musical work from conception to reception. Considers both the
intentions of the composer and the work's acquired cultural meaning and
significance.

Fantasie

343.   Schachter, Carl. "Chopin's Fantasy, op. 49: The Two-Key Scheme."
        In *Chopin Studies,* ed. Jim Samson, 221–253. See 299.

Analyzes the work's complex and highly original tonal structure.
The author supports A-flat major as the main tonic and discusses the purpose of the two-key scheme. Utilizes a Schenkarian approach. Shows
the form of the work as a "march" and three cycles or chains of linked
phrases.

344.   Tomaszewski, Mieczysław. "Fantasie F moll, op. 49—Genre,
        Struktur, Rezeption." *Chopin Studies* 5 (1995): 210–223.

Relates the fantasy to improvisation. Reviews the form, considering disintegrating and integrating aspects. Discusses the reception history of the work and its relation to Polish music.

Impromptus

345.   Barbag-Drexler, Irena. "Die Impromptus von Fryderyk Chopin."
        Chopin Jahrbuch, 1970: 25–108.

Provides a general history of the genre, tracing the impromptu
from the baroque period through the work of other nineteenth-century
composers. Gives a systematic analysis of the Fantaisie-Impromptu, op.

66, and Impromptu in A-flat, op. 29. Considers the melody, rhythm, harmony, form, and piano texture.

Mazurkas

346. Belotti, Gastone. "L'asimmetria ritmica nella mazurca chopiniana." *Nuova rivista musicale italiana* 5, no. 4 (1971): 657–668; no. 5: 827–846.

Provides some background into the study of rhythm in Chopin's music. Gives consideration to the Mazurka, op. 33, no. 3, in different meters. Other works are analyzed in a similar manner.

347. Biegański, Krzysztof. "Évolution de l'attitude de Chopin à l'égard du folklore (suivant ses mazurkas)." In *The Book of the First Musicological Congress Devoted to the Works of Frederick Chopin,* ed. Zofia Lissa, 95–99. See 493.

Discusses the folk mazurka and traces folk elements through all the mazurkas in Chopin's list of works. Considers harmonic and melodic elements, as well as the mazurka rhythm. Divides the stylistic evolution of the mazurkas into three stages.

348. DiMauro, Graziella. "Chopin's Controversial Mazurka, op. 17, no. 4, 'Little Jew.'" *Journal of Jewish Music and Liturgy* 11 (1988–1989): 53–64.

Provides background information on the Mazurka, op. 17, and the source of the pseudonym. Places the meaning of the subtitle in the context of nineteenth-century culture. Probes the folklore elements in op. 17 and Jewish references in early Chopin biographies. Rejects the idea that there is a Jewish influence on the music.

349. Miketta, Janusz. *Mazurki Chopina* [Chopin's mazurkas]. Analizy i objaśnienia dzieł wszystkich Fryderyka Chopina 1. Kraków: Polskie Wydawnictwo Muzyczne, 1949. 470 p.

Analyzes each of Chopin's mazurkas, placing an emphasis on tonality, harmony, and phrasing. Short musical examples support the descriptive analysis.

350.   Nowik, Wojciech. "Próba rekonstrukcji Mazurka F moll, op. 68, nr 4, Fryderyka Chopina" [A trial reconstruction of the Mazurka in F minor, op. 68, no. 4, of F. Chopin]. *Rocznik Chopinowski* (1969): 44–85.

Discusses the sources and available information about the piece. Analyzes the autograph manuscripts and provides photographic plates of manuscripts. Discerns the composer's intentions through extensive musical examples. Relates these examples to the form of the work. Discusses different versions and editions of the mazurka.

351.   Thomson, William. "Functional Ambiguity in Musical Structures." *Music Perception* 1, no. 1 (Fall 1983): 3–27.

Begins with a definition of functional ambiguity. Builds from the view that music is nonreferential, but hierarchical. Tests these ideas on the Mazurka, op. 17, no. 4.

352.   Viljoen, Nical. "The Drone Bass and Its Implications for the Tonal Voiceleading Structure in Two Selected Mazurkas by Chopin." *Indiana Theory Review* 6, no. 1–2 (Fall 1982–Winter 1983): 17–35.

Begins with a Schenkarian focus on voice leading in Chopin's music. Studies the mazurkas to assess the relative importance of tonal voice leading and folk elements, particularly the drone bass, in the music. Provides measure by measure analyses of Mazurkas, op. 6, no. 2, and op. 56, no. 2.

353.   Woźniak, Jolanta. "Melika mazurów Chopina" [Melody in Chopin's Mazurkas]. *Rocznik Chopinowski* 11 (1978): 7–48.

Begins with a review of the research on Chopin's melodies. Uses statistical methods to study melodies, especially intervals and their succession. Eight mazurkas are analyzed: B-flat major (1825); op. 7, no. 2; op. 17, no. 3; op. 24, no. 4; op. 41, no. 1; op. 56, no. 1; op. 63, no. 2; and op. 68, no. 4. The analysis uses equations, graphs, and tables to present a quantitative analysis of the mazurka melodies.

Nocturnes

354. Kirsch, Winfried. "Languido. Religioso zu Chopins Nocturnes in G moll, op. 15, nr. 3, und op. 37, nr. 1." *Chopin Studies* 5 (1995): 105–119.

These are the only Chopin works to use these tempo markings. Probes the meaning of the terms and compares them to visual illustrations. Focuses on the chorale sections of the works.

355. Mainka, Jürgen. "Zu Chopins H Dur Nocturno, opus 32, nr. 1: Ein Aspekt der Tonsprache Chopins in ihrem Verhältnis zur deutschen Romantik." *Beiträge zur Musikwissenschaft* 22, no. 4 (1980): 309–316.

Investigates musical relationships among the nocturne, the B-flat minor sonata, and the "Melodia" text by Zygmunt Krasiński. There is also a connection to Schubert illuminated in the article. The research exhibits a Marxist approach.

356. Rink, John. "Structural Momentum and Closure in Chopin's Op. 9, no. 2." *Chopin Studies* 5 (1995): 82–104.

Synthesizes a view of the work's structure from other analysts. Compares the work to other early works of Chopin and the nocturnes of John Field to explain the piece's idiocyncracies. Supports the discussion with extensive musical examples.

357. Salzer, Felix. "Chopin Nocturne in C-sharp minor, op. 27, no. 1." *Music Forum* 2 (1970): 283–297.

Reduces the music to Schenkarian graphs at different levels and uses this analytical technique to understand the asymmetry of the ternary form. Provides many examples of the music in graphic form.

Polonaises

358. Newcomb, Anthony. "The Polonaise-Fantasy and Issues of Musical Narrative." *Chopin Studies 2,* ed. John Rink and Jim Samson, 84–101. See 300.

Applies the approach of narrative meaning to the form of the work. Explains narrativity in instrumental music and its application to specific Chopin works. Makes reference to four internal musical aspects suggesting a narrative interpretation to the Polonaise-Fantasy. Refers to manuscript studies and other analyses.

359.   Rink, John. "Chopin i Schenker: Improwizacja a struktura" [Chopin and Schenker: Improvisation and Structure]. *Rocznik Chopinowski* 19 (1987): 163–176.

Investigates the influence of improvisation on the structure of a musical work. Applies Schenkarian analysis, relating Schenker's view of improvisation. Applies the theoretical methods to the Polonaise-Fantasy, op. 61. Musical examples.

360.   Samson, Jim. "The Composition-Draft of the Polonaise-Fantasy: The Issue of Tonality." *Chopin Studies,* ed. Jim Samson, 41–58. See 299.

Combines a study of the structure of the work with its genesis as revealed in the composition-draft. Probes Chopin's creativity and working methods. Samson explains broad cultural theories and their applications to specific musical compositions. Uses voice-leading graphs to outline the tonal structure of the Polonaise-Fantasy. Compares the drafts to the final tonal layout in order to speculate on Chopin's creative process.

361.   Tarasti, Eero. "Zu einer Narratologie Chopins." In *Musik-Konzepte 45 Fryderyk Chopin,* ed. Heinz-Klaus Metzger and Rainer Riehn, 58–79. München: Text + Kritik, 1985.   ISBN 3883771988   ML 410.C54 F78 1985

Considers a semiotic perspective of Chopin as a romantic composer. Considers op. 61 by reviewing other writings about the piece, especially commenting about the psychology of the work. Provides a semiotic analysis of op. 61.

Preludes

362.   Agawu, V. Kofi. "Concepts of Closure and Chopin's Opus 28." *Music Theory Spectrum* 9 (1987): 1–17.

Concentrates on analyzing the middle to end of a musical work, assessing closure or the tendency to close. Systematically discusses the concept of closure and borrows definitions from poetry. Considers examples from Chopin's op. 28. Uses Schenkarian graphs to illustrate. Selects examples to present different approaches and methods of closure.

363. Belotti, Gastone. "Il problema della date dei preludi di Chopin." *Revista italiana di Musicologia* 5 (1970): 159–215.

Offers a response to the article by Brown (34) on the dating of the Preludes, op. 28. Reviews the history of research on the collection. Produces a chronological ordering of the preludes, dating from 1831 to 1839.

364. Chomiński, Józef. *Preludia Chopina* [Chopin's Preludes]. Kraków: Polskie Wydawnictwo Muzyczne, 1950. Analizy i objaśnienia dzieł wszystkich Fryderyka Chopina 9. 347 p.   MT 92.C57 t. 9

Analyzes each individual prelude and further considers op. 28 as a cycle. Concludes with general research on the Chopin preludes and their characteristics. Gives a descriptive analysis of the pieces with short musical examples.

365. Eigeldinger, Jean-Jacques. "Twenty-four Preludes, op. 28: Genre, Structure, Significance." In *Chopin Studies,* ed. Jim Samson, 167–193. See 299.

366. Eigeldinger, Jean-Jacques. "Les Vingt-quatre Préludes, op. 28, de Chopin: Genre, structure, signification." *Revue de musicologie* 75, no. 2 (1989): 201–221.

Approaches the preludes as solutions to artistic problems. In studying the individual works, the author attempts to uncover the implicit problems. Provides a history of keyboard preludes, the background to Chopin's op. 28, and the collection's tradition in piano literature, especially with regard to pedagogical purposes. Further discusses the influence of Bach as related to the Études, opp. 10 and 25.

367. Eigeldinger, Jean-Jacques. "Le prélude «de la goutte d'eau» de Chopin. État de la question et essai d'interpretation." *Revue de musicologie* 61, no. 1 (1975): 70–90.

Traces this pseudonym from George Sand and the interpretation of Chopin scholars such as Brown. Classifies writers through their belief in Prelude 6 or 15 as the "raindrop" prelude. Discusses the merits of each choice. The conclusions were reconsidered in 368.

368.   Eigeldinger, Jean-Jacques. "L'achèvement des Préludes, op. 28, de Chopin." *Revue de musicologie* 75, no. 2 (1989): 229–242.

Examines three autograph manuscripts of op. 28. Decides that eight pieces of the set were created in Majorca, and four others were revised there. Describes the manuscripts. Provides an English summary of article.

369.   Hoyt, Reed J. "Chopin's Prelude in A minor Revisited: The Issue of Tonality." *In Theory Only* 8, no. 6 (April 1985): 7–16.

Reviews the analytical work on this prelude by Heinrich Schenker, Leonard B. Meyer, and Michael R. Rogers, finding common ground among the analyses. Discusses the prelude as representing a harmonic process directed to the tonic from a region that does not normally make an immediate connection with the tonic chord.

370.   Hoyt, Reed J. "Harmonic Process, Melodic Process, and Interpretive Aspects of Chopin's Prelude in G minor." *Indiana Theory Review* 5, no. 3 (Spring 1982): 22–42.

Detailed analysis using the implication-realization model. Discusses harmony with figured-bass terminology. Finds noncongruence between harmonic and melodic processes.

371.   Kramer, Lawrence. "Romantic Meaning in Chopin's Prelude in A minor." *19th Century Music* 9, no. 2 (1985): 145–155.

Considers the ambiguity in the pieces as traits of romanticism. Analyzes structural tropes. Interprets relations of melody and harmony, contrast, incongruity, and dissonance.

372.   Kielian-Gilbert, Marianne. "Motive Transfer in Chopin's A Minor Prelude." *In Theory Only* 9, no. 1 (1986): 21–32.

Counters the Hoyt analysis (see 369) by considering the motivic relationships on the surface of the piece, as recognized by Schenker. Defends the Schenkerian approach and expands the analysis.

373. Schachter, Carl. "Rhythmic and Linear Analysis, Durational Reduction." *Music Forum* 5 (1980): 197–232.

Applies analytical techniques to the Prelude, op. 28, no. 3. Provides a Schenkerian style graph with the note values corresponding to the rhythm of the music, rather than structural levels.

Rondo

374. Bronarski, Louis. "Quelques considerations au sujet du rondo pour deux pianos de Chopin." *Chopin Jahrbuch* (1963): 16–25.

Gives background information on the piece from references to Chopin's letters. Compares the version for one and two pianos. Provides performance notes.

Scherzos

375. Chechlińska, Zofia. "Scherzo as a Genre—Selected Problems." *Chopin Studies* 5 (1995):165–173.

Considers the meanings of scherzo as a genre; compares to scherzos of multipartite works. Investigates the common traits of Chopin scherzos. Focuses on "sudden contrasts" as a common element in Chopin's scherzos.

376. Busch-Salmen, Gabriele."Bemerkungen zu den Flötenbearbeitingen der Werke Frédéric Chopins." *Chopin Studies* 5 (1995): 224–234.

Presents various arrangements for flute of Chopin melodies and the place of these works in the literature for flute.

377. Nowik, Wojciech. "Fryderyk Chopin's Scherzo in B minor, op. 20: Form and Thematic Process." *Chopin Studies* 5 (1995): 174–189.

Considers the general structure of the music as a hybrid form. Discusses the genre as a vehicle for innovation. Relates the work to Chopin's biography. Provides a score with intervallic structures (cells) marked.

378.   Rosen, Charles. "Influence: Plagiarism and Inspiration." *19th Century Music* 4, no. 2 (1980): 87–100.

Studies Brahms musical references to the Chopin Scherzos. Discusses the act of quotation versus adaption in the connections between musical works.

379.   Tuchowski, Andrzej. "Scherzo in C-Sharp minor—The Problem of Structural Consistency and Motivic Transformation." *Chopin Studies* 5 (1995): 190–197.

Begins with an interpretation of the introduction. Musical examples isolate motivic cells throughout the work.

Sonatas

380.   Chomiński, Józef. "Sonaty Chopina." *Studia musicologica* 3–5.

Studies national elements in the sonatas. Considers each work while making comparisons to the music of other composers. Much of the text is descriptive analysis.

381.   Nowik, Wojciech. "Sonata C moll, op. 4, Fryderyka Chopina—pomiędzy akademizmem a prekursorstwem" [The Sonata in C minor, op. 4, of F. Chopin—between Academic and Forerunner]. *Rocznik Chopinowski* 21 (1995): 80–114.

An extensive musical analysis considers each movement of the cycle. Reconsiders deviations from the standard structure or accepted practice of the sonata as innovations in the form. Notes that the work was written in Chopin's student years.

382.   Rosen, Charles. "Rehearings: The First Movement of Chopin's Sonata in B-flat minor, op. 35." *19th Century Music* 14, no. 1 (1990): 60–66.

Discusses a mistake in most editions regarding placement of the repeat of the exposition at measure 5. Supports placing the repeat at the beginning by studying internal concerns of the music. Places the work in Chopin's approach to the sonata.

383.   Rudziński, Witold and Mieczysława Demska-Trębacz. "Rytmiczne właściwości tematu głównego w Sonacie B moll Chopina"

[Rhythmic characterization of the main theme in the Sonata in B minor of Chopin]. In *Studia musicologica aesthetica,* ed. Elżbieta Dziębowska, 385–394. Kraków: Polskie Wydawnictwo Muzyczne, 1979. 441 p.   ML 55.L52 1979

Studies the rhythm and stress patterns in the themes of the sonata. Considers the performance of rhythmic ambiguity. Uses numerous statistical charts and graphs.

Songs

384. Matracka-Kościelny, Alicja. "Związki słowno-muzyczne w pieśniach Chopina." *Rocznik Chopinowski* 13 (1981): 29–36.

385. Matracka-Kościelny, Alicja. "The Relationship between Words and Music in Chopin's Songs." *Chopin Studies* 2 (1987): 63–70.

Begins with a review of the relevant literature. Analyzes the phrase structure and meter of the music. Provides a quantitative table of structural elements. Utilizes some musical examples to support the text.

386. Nowik, Wojciech. "Pierścień: zafałszowany klejnot chopinowskiej liryki" [A ring—the falsified jewel of Chopin's lyric]. *Rocznik Chopinowski* 16 (1984): 67–89.

Provides a publication history and analysis of autograph versions of the song.

Other Compositions

387. Prosnak, Jan. "Wariacje fletowe Chopina." *Studia muzykologiczne* 1 (1953): 267–307.

Begins with the background of the piece. Studies each variation and compares it to other pieces with similar intervals and motives. Assesses the authenticity of the composition.

388. Zagiba, Franz. "Eine unbekannte Fassung Chopins Rondeau, op 1." *Chopin Jahrbuch* (1963): 75–79.

Considers the known circumstances in the creation of op. 1 and its publication history. Discusses the version for piano–four hands as Hausmusik, published in Warsaw and Leipzig as "Souvenir à Varsovie."

STYLE STUDIES

389.   Abraham, Gerald. *Chopin's Musical Style*. London: Oxford University Press, 1939. 116 p. Reprint, Westport, Conn.: Greenwood Press, 1980.   ISBN 0313222517   ML 410.C54 A6

A critical review of Chopin's music to assess the development of his musical style. Comments on samples of pieces, rather than presenting analyses of each individual work. Relates Chopin's compositions to the works of other composers. The book reveals Abraham's knowledge of the music, but presents a subjective view of Chopin's musical style. Chopin's oeuvre is divided into three style periods:
Evolution of musical personality, 1822–1831,
Mature style, 1831–1840, and
Last phase, 1841–1849.
Includes short musical examples.

390.   Belotti, Gastone. *Saggi sull'arte e sull'opera di F. Chopin*. Miscellanee saggi convegni, 12. Bologna, 1977. 458 p.

Presents research on a variety of Chopin topics. Covers the general characteristics of Chopin's works and Italian influences seen in rubato and bel canto. Detailed attention is given to the Preludes and Polonaises, opp. 22 and 26. Incorporates short musical examples.

391.   Dziębowska, Elżbieta. "Chopin—romantyk, klasyk, modernista" [Chopin—romantic, classic, modernist]. In *Szkice o kulturze muzycznej XIX wieku* 2, 7–20. Warszawa: Polskie Wydawnictwo Naukowe, 1973.   ML 297.4 S95

The classification of Chopin as a romanticist derives from commentaries by others, and not the composer's personal expression on the arts. The Chopin correspondence relates a more restrained view of the composer. Although the national character of the music relates to romanticism, Chopin's form and balance are charactersitic of classicism. Chopin's experimentation with the composer's musical sound leads to his association with modernism. English summary on pages 287–289.

392.   Dziębowska, Elżbieta. "O polskiej szkole narodowej." *Szkice of kulturze muzycznej XIX wieku*. Warszawa: Polskie Wydawnictwo Naukowe, 1971. 13–32.   ML 297.4 S95

393. Dziębowska, Elżbieta. "On the Polish National School." *Polish Musicological Studies* 2. Kraków: Polskie Wydawnictwo Muzyczne, 1986: 128–148.

Reviews the historiography of "national schools" and nationalism in music. Discusses nineteenth-century Poland and the place of Chopin, especially his taking advantage of folk creativity. Makes a case for Chopin, Moniuszko, and Oskar Kolberg as the essence of the Polish national school.

394. Chechlińska, Zofia. "Chopin a impresjonizm" [Chopin and Impressionism]. In *Szkice o kulturze muzycznej XIX wieku* 2. Warszawa: Polskie Wydawnictwo Naukowe, 1973, 21–34.

Investigates connections between the styles of Chopin and Debussy. Takes the discussion beyond the harmonic elements of Chopin's music to include the influence of Chopin on Debussy, nineteenth-century traditions of piano music, and specific musical elements.

395. Chechlińska, Zofia. *Wariacje i technika wariacyjna w twórczości Chopina* [Variations and variation technique in the creations of Chopin]. Kraków: Musica Jagiellonica, 1995. 198 p. ISBN 8390990282

Studies variation techniques as used in the literature of the nineteenth and twentieth centuries, and applies these to Chopin's music. Considers melody, harmony, texture, and thematic development. Analyzes micro- and macro-structures. Includes an extensive bibliography, an index of works, and index of names.

396. Chomiński, Józef Michał. "Die Evolution des Chopinschen Stils." In *The Book of the First Musicological Congress Devoted to the Works of Frederick Chopin,* ed. Zofia Lissa, 44–52. See 493.

Chopin's music exhibits a personal style, national style, and romantic style. Divides Chopin's work life into three periods: 1810–1830, 1830–1839, and 1839–1849. Considers the changes of each period and overall development of Chopin's melody and harmony.

397. Colombati, Claudia. "W poszukiwaniu poetyki Chopina." [In Search of Chopin's Aesthetics]. *Rocznik Chopinowski* 9 (1975): 9–37.

A discussion of Chopin's aesthetics. Places the composer's music in the context of romanticism.

398.   Gołąb, Maciej, ed. *Przemiany stylu Chopina* [Transformational
        changes in Chopin's style]. Kraków: Musica Jagellonica, 1993.
        198 p.   ML 410.C54 P88 1993.   ISBN 8370990037

Reports of research conducted from 1990 to 1992 at the Musicology Institute of Warsaw University. The articles were presented at a conference in March 1992. The essays cover Chopin's work by genre, with
investigations concentrating on tonality, syntax, and form. English summaries of essays.

399.   Kallberg, Jeffrey. "Chopin's Last Style," *Journal of the American
        Musicological Society* 38, no. 2 (1985): 264–315. See *Rocznik
        Chopinowski* 18 (1989): 17–61.

Chopin's critical reassessment of his craft after 1842 led to aesthetic renewal in his last style period. Concentrates on the Polonaise-
Fantaisie, op. 61, and the Mazurka in F minor, op. 68, no. 4. Gives
background and analysis of the works with a discussion of the sketches.
Underscores Chopin's stylistic experimentation.

400.   Łobaczewska, Stefania. "Fryderyk Chopin." In *Z dziejów pol-
        skiej kultury muzycznej* [From the history of Polish musical cul-
        ture]. Vol. 2, Od Oświecenia do Młodiej Polski [From the
        Enlightenment to Young Poland], 153–236. Kraków: Polskie
        Wydawnictwo Muzyczne, 1966. 703 p.   ML 306.Z15

Approaches Chopin as a representative of romanticism in music.
Makes a point to discuss the tradition from which Chopin emerged, including other pianist-composers, the classical style, and contact with
folk music. Goes through each genre of Chopin's music with references
to specific works, but no musical examples. Considers Chopin as a representative of nationalism in Polish music.

401.   Reiss, Józef. "Geniusz Chopina" [Chopin's Genius]. Chap. 11 in
        Najpiękniejsz ze wszystkich jest muzyka polska [The most beau-
        tiful of all is Polish music]. Kraków: T. Giesdzczykiewicz, 1946.
        264 p.

Considers Chopin's creations to be revolutionary. Inflates the importance of Chopin in music history to confirm that Polish music is the
most beautiful.

402. Sandelewski, Wiarosław. "Contributi italiani sugli studi su Chopin." In *Chopin in Italia,* 75–92. Accademie Polacca delle Scienze, Conference e Studi, 72. Wrocław: Zakład Narodowy imienia Ossolińskich Wydawnictwo PAN, 1977. 92 p.   ML 410.C54 B23

Reviews the publication history of research on Chopin by Italian scholars. Includes translations and editions of books in other languages.

403. Stegemann, Michael. "Die beiden Gesichter der Nacht: Nocturne und Scherzo in der französischen Musik und Literatur von 1830 bis 1850." *Chopin Studies* 5 (1995):158–164.

Considers the nocturne and scherzo as program music. Relates the genres to the night and to literature of the period. Provides a chart with the chronology of relevant musical and literary works.

Dynamics

404. Turło, Dalila. "The Evolution of Dynamics as an Element of Construction in Chopin's Works." *Annales Chopin* 6 (1961–1964): 90–103.

Studies dynamics as related to sound, motivic development, and thematic development beginning with the Chopin manuscripts. Discusses the progression of dynamic use throughout Chopin's career and Chopin's ways of manipulating the basic dynamic effect. No use of musical examples to support text.

Harmony

405. Eibner, Franz. "Über die Akkorde im Satz Chopins." *Chopin Jahrbuch* (1970): 3–24.

Studies the relation of phrasing and chord structures, particularly their consonance and dissonance. Analyzes musical examples using Schenkarian techniques.

406. Matter, Jean. "De l'harmonie complémentaire et de l'expression du dépaysement dans la musique de Chopin." *Schweizerische Musikzeitung* 101, no. 2 (March–April 1961): 93–97.

Discusses third relations in Chopin's music. Compares the harmonic techniques to Delacroix's use of complementary colors.

Melody

407. Koszewski, Andrzej. "Melodyka walców Chopina" [The melodies of Chopin's waltzes]. *Studia muzykologiczne* 2 (1953): 276–341.

An extended study on melody. Refers to other studies of Chopin melody. Reviews the waltzes by period and presents a descriptive analysis. Compares Chopin's work to that of other nineteenth-century composers and folk sources. Incorporates many short musical examples.

408. Ottich, Maria. "Chopins Klavierornamentik." *Annales Chopin* 3 (1958): 7–62.

Covers all aspects of the composer's melodic style, including figuration, ornamentation, rhythm, and harmony. Addresses the form and function of melodic patterns. Considers the influence of bel canto on Chopin's melodies. Uses musical examples.

Rhythm and Meter

409. Belotti, Gastone. *Le origini italiane del „rubato" Chopiniano.* Wrocław: Ossolińskich, 1968. 42 p.

The historical overview of the concept of rubato extends back to Casteglione. Discusses the dissemination of Italian music to Poland and Italian influences on Chopin. The research is supported with short musical examples and references to Chopin's letters.

410. Dahlig, Ewa. "Z badań nad rytmikę polskich tańców ludowych: mazurek, kujawiak, chodzony a „Mazurki" Chopina" [From research on the rhythm of the Polish folk dances mazurek, kujawiak, and chodzony, and the mazurkas of Chopin]. *Muzyka* 39, no. 3 (1994): 105–130.

Produces extensive charts and statistics on the dance rhythms in the music. Differentiates the rhythms of the various dances. Analyzes folk sources and makes comparisons to the Chopin mazurkas. Concludes that the Chopin works relate closely to vocal models of the folk dances.

411. Belotti, Gastone. "Die rhythmische Asymmetrie in den Mazurken von Chopin." *Chopin Jahrbuch* (1970): 109–137.

Relates the mazurka rhythm to rubato. Studies the connection between metric ambiguity and folk origins of the mazurka. Provides extensive notes.

412. Hlawiczka, Karol. "L'échange rythmique dans la musique de Chopin." *Annales Chopin* 4 (1959): 39–50.

Considers rhythmic exchange as a source of rhythmic dissonance in Chopin. Many short musical examples show excerpts of superimposed rhythmic patterns.

413. Hlawiczka, Karl. "Eine rhythmische Analyse der Ges-dur-Etüde von Chopin, op. 10, nr. 5." *Chopin Jahrbuch* 1 (1956): 123–131.

Considers the rhythm of note values, dynamics, melody, meter, and harmony. Gives different analyses of figuration.

414. Kholopov, Yuri. "Aufzeichnungen der Chopins Metrik." *Chopin Studies* 5 (1995): 245–261.

Investigates meter and accent in Chopin's musical phrases. Refers to many musical examples. Provides a micro- and macro-analysis of meter, which are applied to genres such as the scherzos and nocturnes.

415. Koszewski, Andrzej. "Problemy rytmiczne i agogiczne w walcach Chopina" [Rhythmic and Agogic Problems in the Waltzes of Chopin]. *Annales Chopin* 3 (1958): 113–132.

Discusses the rhythm and accent pattern of the waltz. Shows how the rhythm is formed into phrases. Variants in tempo among Chopin's waltzes are addressed. Numerous musical examples are used to support ideas. Summary in German.

Texture

416. Frączkiewicz, Aleksander. "Faktura fortepianowa koncertów Fryderyka Chopina" [The piano texture of the concertos of F. Chopin]. *Annales Chopin* 3 (1958): 133–158.

Analyzes bass lines, chord textures, melodic figuration, the separate hand parts, and the use of pedal in Chopin's concertos. Some use of musical examples, although a greater number of references is made to specific measures in the scores.

417.   Lissa, Zofia. "Faktura fortepianowa Beethovena a Chopina" [The
        piano textures of Beethoven and Chopin]. *Muzyka* 15, no. 4
        (1970): 42–66.

Uses a number of examples to assess the influence of Beethoven
on Chopin. Compares works in different genres to show similarities in
piano texture.

Timbre and Instrumentation

418.   Abraham, Gerald. "Chopin and the Orchestra." In *The Book of
        the First Musicological Congress Devoted to the Works of Fred-
        erick Chopin,* ed. Zofia Lissa, 85–87. See 493.

The author modifies the view originally expressed in *Chopin's
Musical Style* (see 389) regarding Chopin's inaptitude at treating the orchestra. Places Chopin's orchestra in the context of his models, especially the composers Elsner and Kurpiński.

419.   Chechlińska, Zofia. "Zakres materiału dźwiękowegoi i jego dys-
        pozycja w utworach Chopina" [The range of sound material and
        its disposition in Chopin's works]. *Muzyka* 14, no. 1 (1969):
        54–62.

Discusses Chopin's use of the keyboard. Divides works into
groups based on keyboard style.

Ballades

420.   Lisecki, Wiesław. "Ballada F. Chopina—Inspiracje literackie czy
        muzyczne?" [F. Chopin's ballades—literary or musical inspira-
        tion?]. *Rocznik Chopinowski* 19 (1987): 247–258.

421.   Lisecki, Wiesław. "Die Ballade von Frédéric Chopin—Litarar-
        ische oder musikalische Inspiration?" *Chopin Studies* 3 (1990):
        305–317.

Discusses the relation of music to narrative and literary work.
Chopin related the ballad to dance. The author applies this theory to specific works. Musical examples, especially long excerpts from the G-
minor Ballade. Relates Chopin and Mickiewicz.

422. Parakilas, James. *Ballads Without Words: Chopin and the Tradition of the Instrumental* Ballade. Portland, Or.: Amadeus Press, 1992. 358 p.   ISBN 0931340470   ML 460.P34 1992

Review: Nicholas Temperly, *Notes* 50, no. 3 (March 1994): 964–965.

Explores the origin of the ballade as a narrative model, especially the historical background and ballade as a national reference. Discusses the essential features of the literary ballads that Chopin could have known, including those of Mickiewicz. The chapter on Chopin's ballade form examines musical structures and considers the extent to which they correspond to narrative structures. Discusses the overall rhythm, melodic character, transformation of themes, structure, and sonata elements through musical examples. Much of the book discusses ballades by other composers. Includes a bibliography, index, chronology of works, and discography.

Études

423. Brody, Elaine and Jan LaRue. "Trois nouvelles études." *Musical Quarterly* 72, no. 1 (1986): 1–15.

Discusses three études composed for Fétis and Moscheles. The sequence of the three works was not set, but they appear as published in the *Méthode de Méthodes*. Provides biographical information on Moscheles, Fétis, and the publisher Schlesinger. Discusses the pianistic aspects of the music, contrasting the works with the Études op. 10 and op. 25.

Impromptus

424. Samson, Jim. "Impromptu Fis dur Chopina" [The impromptu in F-sharp major of Chopin]. *Rocznik Chopinowski* 19 (1987): 237–246.

425. Samson, Jim. "Chopin's F-sharp Impromptu—Notes on Genre, Style and Structure." *Chopin Studies* 3 (1990): 297–304.

Considers the genre, style, and structure of this work. Provides historical perspective to the impromptu as a genre and makes connections between Chopin works. Relates the style and structure of the F-sharp major Impromptu to other Chopin compositions. This piece signals a change in Chopin's style. Argues that the force-field between genre and style has subverted structure.

Mazurkas

426.   Asafvev, B. "Mazurki Shopena" [Chopin's mazurkas]. *Sovetskaia Muzyka* 2, no. 3 (1947): 61–76.

Concentrates on the folk characteristics of the mazurkas. Addresses specific works, especially with regard to form and rhythm. Provides only a few musical examples.

427.   Swartz, Anne. "Folk Dance Elements in Chopin's Mazurkas." *Journal of Musicological Research* 4, no. 3–4 (1983): 417–426.

Compares folk mazurkas with Chopin's compositions in this genre. Considers the mazur, kujawiak, and oberek. Matches each type with examples in Chopin's music, discussing characteristics of each. The folk references are taken from Oskar Kolberg's multivolume collection.

Nocturnes

428.   Branson, David. *John Field and Chopin.* New York: St. Martin's Press, 1972. 216 p.   ML 410.F445 B7 1972b

Reviews the literature on the Chopin-Field influence and compares the music through examples. Also investigates Hummel's influence on Chopin. The study was stimulated by critical comments in biographies of Chopin, such as that by Niecks (see 71). Contains an index, bibliography, and list of Field's compositions.

429.   Methuen-Campbell, James. "John Field and Chopin—Similarities and Differences in Their Approach to the Nocturne Genre." *Chopin Studies* 5 (1995):120–125.

Expands the comparison of Chopin and Field as viewed by Branson (428). Writers have not focused on their shared stylistic traits. Discusses the difficulty in identifying a common nocturne model. Looks closely at the melody-accompaniment relationship.

430.   Turło, Teresa Dalila. "Transcriptions des nocturnes de Chopin comme forme particulière de réception de la lyrique instrumentale." *Chopin Studies* 5 (1995): 153–157.

Discusses arrangements for different instruments as a consideration of reception history. Illuminates the rich arrangement literature derived from Chopin's works.

Piano Trio

431. Chodkowski, Andrzej. "Kilka uwag o Trio fortepianowym Fryderyka Chopina" [A few notes about the piano trio of F. Chopin]. *Rocznik Chopinowski* 14 (1982): 13–20.

Relates the trio to the other chamber works of Chopin, which are important because they show the composer's approach to composing for instruments. Reviews the creation of the piano trio and notes the influences of Elsner and other Polish composers of the period.

Preludes

432. Wiora, Walter. "Über den geistigen Zusammenhang der Präludien und Etüden Chopins." *Musik des Ostens* 1(1962): 76–79.

Considers the Preludes, op. 28, as a romantic reflection of Bach's prelude cycles. Discusses the Études, opp. 10 and 25, as cycles.

Sonatas

433. Chołopow, Jurij. "O zasadach kompozycji Chopina: zagadka finału Sonaty B-moll." [About the foundations of Chopin's composition: the enigma of the finale of the B-minor sonata]. *Rocznik Chopinowski* 19 (1987): 211–235.

434. Chołopow, Jurij. "Über die kompositionsgrundsätze bei Frederic Chopin: Das Rätsel des Finales der Sonate B moll." *Chopin Studies* 3 (1990): 269–295.

Studies the style and conceptions of the movement in detail, relating the analysis to studies by Rieman, Leichtentritt, Bronarski, and Benara. Covers the harmony, themes and motives, modulations and key relations, and form. Presents graphs and charts to reduce musical concepts.

Songs

435. Kaczyński, Tadeusz. "Texte poètique—en tant que source d'inspiration musicale dans certain chants de Chopin et de Moniuszko." In *The Book of the First Musicological Congress Devoted to the Works of Frederick Chopin,* ed. Zofia Lissa, 313–318. See 493.

Discusses and compares textual-musical relations in three song settings common to Chopin and Moniuszko: "Bacchanale" of Stefan

Witwicki; "Le Printemps" of Stefan Witwicki; and "Ma bien aimée" of Adam Mickiewicz. Concentrates on how the expression, versification, and intonation of the texts influenced the music.

436. Swartz, Anne. "Elsner, Chopin, and Musical Narrative as Symbols of the Nation." *Polish Review* 39, no. 4 (1994): 445–456.

Cites Elsner's "Treatise on Meter and Rhythm" as one of the first studies of Polish text to make a nationalistic statement. Discusses the development of art song in nineteenth-century Poland. Places Chopin's songs in the context of nationalism and cultural history. "Chopin and Elsner defined the art song as an effective medium for national artistic expression."

437. Tarnowska-Kaczowrowska, Krystyna. "Pieśni Fryderyka Chopina" [The songs of F. Chopin]. *Rocznik Chopinowski* 19 (1987): 259–296.

Begins with a review of the literature on Chopin songs. Provides notes on each song and plots the literary themes of the song texts. Discusses textual-musical relations and relations to other genres. Gives musical incipits of the song literature. Searches for patterns in key and tempo.

438. Tomaszewski, Mieczysław. "Filiacje twórczości pieśniarskiej Chopina z polską muzyką ludową, popularną i artystyczną" [The descent of Chopin's song creations with Polish folk, popular, and artistic music]. *Muzyka* 6, no. 2 (1961): 79–89.

Analyzes the songs of Chopin and compares them to folk songs and popular music. Classifies nineteenth-century songs by type and provides a context with the work of other composers. Relates the music to the national style of Chopin to reveal a synthesis of musical elements.

Waltzes

439. Zuber, Barbara. "Syndrom des Salon und Autonomie." In *Musik-Konzepte 45 Fryderyk Chopin*, ed. Heinz-Klaus Metzger and Rainer Riehn, 17–51. München: Text + Kritik, 1985. ISBN 3883771988   ML 410.C54 F78 1985

Review: Detlef Gojowy, *Neue Zeitschrift für Musik* 147, no. 9 (September 1986): 80–81.

Discusses the waltzes as salon pieces that reflect the aesthetics of the time. Places the stylized pieces in the context of Chopin's background and life in Paris. Analysis of the waltzes refers to numerous musical examples.

PERFORMANCE TRADITION

440. Kleczynski, Jean. *The Works of Frederic Chopin and Their Proper Interpretation.* Trans. Alfred Whittingham. London: William Reeves, n.d. 76 p.

Publishes the texts of three lectures. Gives notes on performing specific works with fingerings and drawings of hand position. Discusses Chopin's thoughts about technique, developmental exercises, use of pedal, phrasing, and rubato. Includes an index of works referenced.

441. Porte, John F. *Chopin the Composer and His Music.* London: William Reeves, n.d. 193 p.   ML 410.C54 P65

Relates to performing Chopin and the discovery of his style. Reviews the performance traditions and discusses specific pianists. Covers the musical works by genre, weighing the merits of the differing approaches of various pianists. Includes a discographic essay.

442. Szymanowski, Karol. "On Frédéric Chopin (1923)." *Polish Music* 12, no. 3 (1977): 6–9.

Publishes excerpts of the Szymanowski essay on Chopin. The text discusses the Polish character of the music and the composer's place in Polish music.

443. Steglich, Rudolf. "Chopin's Klavier." *Chopin Jahrbuch* (1963): 139–160.

Illuminates instruments specified in concert reviews and other documents of the period. Presents the clavichord of Chopin's youth and the pantaleon. Discusses piano makers of the period and the attributes of various instruments.

444. Frederick, Edmund M. "The Romantic Sound in Four Pianos of Chopin's Era." *19th Century Music* 3, no. 2 (1979): 150–153.

Describes the physical and tonal characteristics of four instruments: Hasska (Viennese grand, 1820s), Stodart (English, c. 1830),

Pleyel (French, c. 1845), and Erard (London, 1856). Matches the sound of each instrument with various styles of music.

Competitions

445. Prosnak, Jan. *Międzynarodowe konkursy pianistyczne imiena Fryderyka Chopina w Warszawie 1927–1970* [The F. Chopin International Piano Competition in Warsaw 1927–1970]. Warszawa: Towarszystwo imiena Fryderyka Chopina, 1970. ML 76.F76 P82

Reviews each contest, providing lists of participants, jury members, and repertory. Includes many photographs of participants, and reproductions of programs, reviews, and posters. Provides detailed results of each competition in the contest's long history.

Chopin as Teacher

The popularity of Chopin's music in modern performance has created a natural interest in his abilities as a teacher. Research on this aspect of the composer's activities has stressed the lineage of performers back to his students.

446. Eigeldinger, Jean-Jacques. *Chopin vu par ses élèves*. Neuchâtel: Éditions de la Baconnière, 1970. 158 p. ML 410.E54 C4913

Reviews: Jeffrey Kallberg, *Notes* 36, no. 3 (1980): 645–646; Tibor Kneif, *Neue Zeitschrift für Musik* 141, no. 4 (1980): 395; Adélaide de Place, *Revue de musicologie* 66, no. 1 (1980): 102–103; Alan Walker, *Music and Letters* 61, no. 3–4 (1980): 436–437; Monika Schwartz, *Österreichische Musikzeitung* 36. No. 1 (1981): 57; Jeffrey Kallberg, *Journal of the American Musicological Society* 42, no. 1 (1989): 189–193; Nicolas Temperley, *Notes* 44, no. 2 (1987): 270–271; Dalila Turło, *Rocznik Chopinowski* 13 (1981): 153–158; Jeanne Holland, *Performance Practice Review* 2, no. 1(Spring 1989): 107–110; Charles Rosen, *New York Review of Books* 34, no. 9 (May 1987): 9–11.

Discusses fundamental piano technique in a broad outline by providing excerpts from the writings of Chopin students. Similarly approaches the interpretation of specific works. Provides a list of source materials and short biographical sketches of Chopin's students.

447. Ullyot, Marianne. "Chopin and Liszt: A Legacy of Teaching." *Journal of the American Liszt Society* 10 (1981): 39–42.

Compares and contrasts the piano teaching of Liszt and Chopin. Discusses each performer's teaching routine and notes the differences of each with the common teaching tradition of the time.

448. Ekier, Jan. "Chopin jako pedagog" [Chopin as a teacher]. *Ruch Muzyczny* 18, no. 10 (May 12, 1974): 15–17; 18, no. 11 (May 26, 1974): 16–18.

Information is gleaned from Chopin correspondence, as well as the comments of Mikuli and other students.

449. Holland, Jeanne. "Technika i jej kształcenie w pedagogice Chopina" [Technique and its formation in the pedagogy of Chopin]. *Rocznik Chopinwski* 11 (1978): 49–74.

Relies on the Chopin correspondence and nineteenth-century literature on the composer to construct a view of his teaching style. Addresses the performer's position at the piano, hand position, and use of fingers. Deduces exercises for students and appropriate literature. Produces a list of literature that refers to Chopin teaching. Gives notes on several individual students.

450. Holland, Jeanne. "Chopin the Teacher." *Journal of the American Liszt Society* 17 (1985): 39–48.

Information provided on the scheduling of lessons, fees, pianos, and teaching style. Synthesizes information from a variety of sources, as represented in the footnotes.

451. Purswell, Joan M. "Chopin as Teacher." *Clavier* 18, no. 7 (1979): 16–19.

Summarizes the available information on Chopin in the role of teacher. Discusses his technical approach to playing the repertoire that he assigned to his students.

452. Bronarski, Ludwik. "Les élèves de Chopin." *Annales Chopin* 6 (1961–1964): 7–12.

Lists the known students of Chopin—32 females and 8 males. Adds other names suggested in the biographical literature on the composer.

453. Jaeger, Bertrand. "Quelques nouveaux noms d'élèves de Chopin." 64, no. 1 (1978): 76–108.

Expands the list of known students from such diverse sources as letters and notes in musical scores. Gives extensive footnotes and documentation. Includes a chronological table of students.

454. Lenz, Wilhelm von. "Chopin." In *The Great Piano Virtuosos of Our Time*, 27–74. Trans. Madeleine R. Baker. New York: Schirmer, 1899. 169 pp.   ML 397.L57 1899

Presents Lenz' personal notes on playing for Chopin. He was introduced to the composer by Franz Liszt. Chopin agreed to give Lenz lessons. Gives comments about Chopin's teaching and about persons encountered while studying with Chopin.

455. Cortot, Alfred. *In Search of Chopin*. Trans. Cyril and Rena Clarke. Westport, Conn.: Greenwood Press, 1975; reprint of New York: Abelard Press, 1952. Translation of *Aspects de Chopin*. 268 p.   ISBN 0837179718   ML 410.C54C603 1975

Discusses Chopin's appearance and his teaching. The book includes a transcription of twelve manuscript sheets of notes for a piano method. Reviews Chopin's references to his music in the letters [according to Opieński edition, see 140]. Explores Chopin's various connections to France, especially the concerts and other programs. Includes a bibliography and discography.

456. Holland, Jeanne. "Chopin's Piano Method." *Piano Quarterly* 33, no. 129 (1985): 32–43.

Gives the background and historical perspective of the composer's writing on teaching. Summarizes each part of the Chopin method and provides explanatory notes on other writers about Chopin's performance style. Provides an annotated list of students.

457. Milsztejn, J. "'Metoda Chopina" [The piano method of Chopin]. *Ruch Muzyczny* 12, no. 12 (June 15–30, 1968): 5–7.

Provides a Polish translation of the text of the piano method taken from the text in Cortot's *Aspects* (See 455).

458. Mycielski, Zygmunt. "Rękopis 'Metody' Chopina" [The manuscript of the piano method of Chopin]. *Ruch Muzyczny* 12, no. 1 (January 1–15, 1968): 3–7.

Discusses the provenance of Chopin's piano method. The manuscript, written in French, belongs to the Robert Owen Lehman Foundation. It was first discussed by Cortot in his *Aspects* (see 455). The article provides a plate from the sixteen-page manuscript.

459. Mycielski, Z. "Jeszcze o rękopsie 'Metody' Chopin w odpowiedzi Jarosławowi Iwaszkiewiczowi" [More about the manuscript of Chopin's piano method in reply to Jaroslaw Iwaszkiewicz]. *Ruch Muzyczny* 12, no. 7 (April 1–15, 1968): 10.

Answers an article published in *Życie Warszawy* (February 11–12, 1968). Reprints excerpts from this newspaper article.

460. Nikołajew, Wiktor. " 'Metoda fortepianowa' Fryderyka Chopina" [The piano method of F. Chopin]. *Ruch Muzyczny* 29, no. 21 (October 13, 1985): 5–7.

Proposes a reordering of the parts of the Method from the outline prepared by Cortot. See 455.

Reception of Music

Perspectives on Chopin and his music have varied greatly over the generations since his time. In many respects, the changing views can be perceived in the references selected for this research guide. Studies in the changing reception of a composer's work is tied to an understanding of cultural history and related to how the music is heard.

461. Samson, Jim. "Chopin Reception: Theory, History, Analysis." In *Chopin Studies 2*, ed. John Rink and Jim Samson, 1–17. See 300.

Begins with a discussion of the theory behind reception studies in music. Studies Chopin reception by sketching four profiles of Chopin that emerged after the composer's death in 1849. Considers French writing on Chopin by examining the context of differing views of Chopin. Publications of works by Breitkopf und Härtel led to inclusion of Chopin's music in the canon. Chopin also influenced the Russian composers of the Balakirev circle. Finally, Chopin is associated with domestic piano performance in the Victorian age. The author further considers Chopin in our own time and the place of reception studies in the "new musicology."

462.   Kallberg, Jeffrey. "Small Fairy Voices: Sex, History and Meaning in Chopin." In *Chopin Studies 2*, ed. John Rink and Jim Samson, 50–71. See 300.

Reviews musicology's attempts to develop interpretations of sexuality and desire in music. Traces the history of references to Chopin. Sexual ambiguity of Chopin stems from angel references, association with George Sand and her daughter Solange, and physical weakness.

463.   Bronarski, Ludwik. *Szkice chopinowski* [Chopin sketches]. Kraków: Polskie Wydawnictwo Muzyczne, 1961. 353 p. Biblioteka Chopinowska 4. *Études sur Chopin.* Lausanne: Éditions la Concorde, 1944.   ML 410.C54 B85

Collected works on Chopin. Subjects include Chopin and literature, salon music, dedications, and Chopin's relations with Italy. Gives reminiscences about Chopin. Few of the studies investigate specific works.

464.   Ballstaedt, Andreas. "Chopin as 'Salon Composer' in Nineteenth-Century German Criticism." In *Chopin Studies 2*, ed. John Rink and Jim Samson, 18–34. See 300.

Discusses nineteenth-century responses to Chopin's music. German reception originated with Schumann and is tied to the salon. Explains the development of the salon and the role of music. Discusses the gender implications of Chopin's music and genres tied to salon performance. The pejorative view of salons led by association to criticism of Chopin's music.

465.   Ludvová, Jitka. "Twórczość Chopina w dziewiętnastowiecznej Pradze" [The creations of Chopin in nineteenth-century Prague]. *Rocznik Chopina* 18 (1989): 107–123.

Chronicles Chopin performances in Prague. Discusses the place of the piano in musical life and the popularity of Chopin's music. Lists performances and performers to 1849.

466. Szczepański, Rafał. "Muzyka i kult Chopina w okupowanej Warszawie" [Music and the Chopin cult in occupied Warsaw]. *Ruch Muzyczny* 33, no. 19 (September 10, 1989): 23–25; no. 20 (September 24, 1989): 3–4.

Describes activities and importance of Chopin's music as a national symbol during World War II. Outlines the move toward private concerts and independent scholarly activities.

PERFORMANCE PRACTICE

Much could be written concerning the performance of Chopin's works that would be completely subjective. Empirical work has addressed a number of performance problems, chiefly the approach to ornaments, pedalling, and tempo rubato.

467. Methuen-Campbell, James. *Chopin Playing: From the Composer to the Present Day.* New York: Taplinger, 1981. 289 p. ISBN 0800815114 ML 410.C54M48

Reviews: Nicolas Temperley, *Musical Times,* no. 1663 (September 1981): 604–605; Robert L. Jacobs, *Music Review* 43, no. 1 (February 1982): 63–64; Zofia Chechlińska, *Rocznik Chopinowski* 16 (1984): 165–170.

This book aims to describe the art of the great Chopin players and to differentiate the subtle differences of approach to Chopin's music. The introduction discusses editions, instruments, and recordings. The work considers Chopin playing, the influence of Liszt and Leschetizky, and then specific pianists by country of origin. The chapter on Chopin himself is compiled from descriptions of his performance style.

Includes biographical data on pianists and assessments from recordings. Provides a list of the pupils of Chopin and prizewinners of the Frederic Chopin International Competition. A discography and bibliography are appended.

468. Kanski, Józef. "Z badań nad interpretacją dzieł Chopina" [From research on the interpretation of Chopin's works]. *Annales Chopin* 4 (1959): 123–135.

Reviews references on how Chopin played his works. Compares versions of the Polonaise in A-flat major, op. 53, by different performers.

Includes a table of metronome markings of different performances. German summary.

469.   Rink, John. "Authentic Chopin: History, Analysis, and Intuition in Performance." *Chopin Studies 2*, ed. John Rink and Jim Samson, 214–244. See 300.

Discusses how a performer might achieve an "authentic interpretation" of Chopin's music. Applies intuition based on familiarity with the composer's style. The author's ideas are applied to several case studies. Includes musical examples and voice-leading graphs.

470.   Kleczynski, Jean. *Chopin's Greater Works: How They Should Be Understood*. Trans. Natalie Janotha. London: William Reeves, 1896. 115 p.

Prints the texts of three lectures that analyze Chopin's works by genre with regard to performance.

471.   Higgins, Thomas. "Chopin's Music and Fashions of Performing It: Some Crucial Differences." *American Music Teacher* 29, no. 4 (1980): 12–14.

Reviews the adherance to all musical markings in the Chopin works most commonly taught. Discusses approaches to part writing, phrasing, pedal, tempo, and ornamentation.

472.   Kiorpes, George. "Chopin's Short Trills and Snaps. An Insoluble Enigma?" *Journal of the American Liszt Society* 13 (1983): 59–72.

Differentiates three notations of this ornament. Examines all ornaments to draw conclusions on proper performance approach. Provides many musical examples from the piano literature.

473.   Dunn, John Petrie. *Ornamentation in the Works of Frederick Chopin*. London: Novello, 1921. Reprinted by Da Capo Press. 75 p. MT 145.D95

Shows how to perform the various ornaments in Chopin's music. Many musical examples are taken from Chopin works. Covers the different types of trills, arpeggios, appogiaturas, pedaling, and other embellishments. Includes an index of quotations from Chopin works.

474. Fritz, Thomas. "How Did Chopin Want His Ornaments Played?" *Rocznik Chopinowski* 17 (1985): 45–52.

Discusses rolled chords preferred on the beat and short trills prefixed with upper neighbor tones.

475. Strauss, John F. "The Puzzle of Chopin's Tempo Rubato." *Clavier* 22, no. 5 (May–June 1983): 22–25.

Reviews the different views of Chopin's approach to rubato passages. Contemporaries noted the flexibility of Chopin's rhythm, whereas this is contradicted by other writers. Concludes that Chopin referred to the performance practice outlined in C.P.E. Bach's *Versuch über die wahre Art das Clavier zu spielen.*

476. Rowland, David. "Chopin's *Tempo Rubato* in Context." In *Chopin Studies 2*, ed. John Rink and Jim Samson, 199–213. See 300.

Presents explanations of this rhythmic flexibility of music in historical context. Discusses Chopin's use of *tempo rubato* in performance and as notated in music. Chopin created an impression of rhythmic flexibility within the framework of strict bar length.

477. Sobieski, Marian and Jadwiga Sobieska. "Tempo rubato u Chopina i w polskiej muzyce ludowej" [Tempo rubato in Chopin and in Polish folk music]. *Muzyka* 5, no. 3 (1960): 30–41.

Discusses the annecdotal background to Chopin's performance of tempo rubato in his works. Adds the historical concept of rubato. Relates the performance tradition to folk music and the performance of dance rhythms. Musical examples compare folk melodies in transcription.

478. Whiteside, Abby. *Mastering the Chopin Etudes and Other Essays*, ed. Joseph Prostakoff and Sophia Rosoff. New York: Charles Scribner's Sons, 1969. 200 p.   ML 60.W4697 M4

This book concerns piano technique. The author believed that the Chopin études are a good source for developing all aspects of piano technique. The title essay, dated June 1952, discusses some individual études by pianistic problem. The second essay is entitled: "Work Sketch for the Chopin Études, June 13, 1953." Incorporates musical examples.

479. Deschaussées, Monique. *Chopin: les 24 études.* Montreal: Louise Courteau, 1986. 157 p.   ISBN 2892390311   ML 410.C54 D37 1986

Review: Jean-Pierre Bartoli, *Analyse musicale* 7 (April 1987): 79–80.

480. Deschaussées, Monique. *Frédéric Chopin: 24 Études—Vers une interprétation.* Fondettes: Éditions Van de Velde, 1995. 158 p. ISBN 2858682240   ML 410.C54 D37 1995

Offers specific notes on the performance of each étude of op. 10 and op. 25. Musical examples illuminate performance problems, suggest fingerings, and provide approaches to phrasing.

481. Kresky, Jeffrey. *A Reader's Guide to the Chopin Preludes.* Westport, Conn.: Greenwood Press, 1994. 130 p.   ISBN 0313292531 ML 410.C54K75 1994

A musical analysis of the Preludes with notes to aid in the appreciation of the pieces. The introduction contemplates the meaning of the title "prelude" and addresses the concept of unity in op. 28.

482. Aprahamian, Felix. "Jan Smeterlin and his Unfinished Book on the Interpretation of Chopin." In *Karol Szymanowski and Jan Smeterlin: Correspondence and Essays,* ed. B.M. Maciejewski and Felix Aprahamian, 104–129. London: Allegro Press, 1969. 160 p.   ML 410.S99 M2

Review: Max Harrison, *Composer* no. 36 (Summer 1970): 32.
Talks of Smeterlin's own approach to the piano and his path to specializing in Chopin. Discusses touch and finger position. Reviews the Preludes, op. 28, with notes on each piece. Underscores the importance of understanding the mazurka as a dance.

483. Shaffer, L. Henry. "Performing the F-sharp Minor Prelude, op. 28, no. 8." In *Chopin Studies 2,* ed. John Rink and Jim Samson, 183–198. See 300.

Utilizes a methodology of comparing computer recordings of four piano performances to extract the meaning of the work. Evaluates performances in terms of technique and grasp of structure and character. Traces durations and dynamics on a graph. Compares to structure of music and markings in the score.

484. Gerig, Reginald R. *Famous Pianists and Their Technique*. Washington: Robert B. Luce, 1974. 540 p.   ML 700.G44

Includes a section on "The Leschetizky Influence" (pp. 271–286). Discusses Leschetizky as pianist and teacher, specific principles of his technique, and famous students.

485. Murray, David. "The Romantic Piano: Chopin to Ravel." In *The Book of the Piano*, ed. Dominic Gill, 78–113. Ithaca, N.Y.: Cornell University Press, 1981.   ISBN 0801413990   ML 650.B54 288 p.

Presents Chopin and his music in the context of other pianists. Considers Chopin and Liszt as the pianistic focus of the romantic period. An essay on Chopin and his music provides a synthesis of information on the composer.

486. Hinson, Maurice. "Pedaling the Piano Works of Chopin." In *The Pianist's Guide to Pedaling*, ed. Joseph Banowetz, 179–198. Bloomington: Indiana University Press, 1985.   ISBN 0253344948 MT 227.B2 1985

The books begins with a history of the piano's pedals, then techniques for the right, middle, and left pedals. The chapter on Chopin discusses pedal markings in autographs and edition markings. Gives many references to specific Chopin pieces. Concludes with general suggestions for pedaling in Chopin's piano music.

487. Palmieri, Robert. *Piano Information Guide: An Aid to Research.* New York: Garland, 1989. 329 p.   ISBN 0824077784   ML 128.P3 P34 1989

An annotated bibliography covering the general history of the instrument. Includes a section on the "Pianos of Specific Composers." Key works on Chopin's music are covered in "Music of Specific Composers."

488. Rowland, David. *A History of Pianoforte Pedalling*. Cambridge: Cambridge University Press, 1993. 194 p.   ISBN 0521402662 MT227.R72 1993

Review: Nicholas Temperly, *Notes* 52, no. 2 (December 1995): 466–468.
Part III studies "Pedalling after c. 1800." A number of references are made to the Chopin-Liszt-Thalberg era. Pages 125–130 specifically

examine Chopin's music through musical examples. Includes an index and bibliography.

SOCIETIES, ARCHIVES, MUSEUMS

The Chopin Society in Warsaw, Towarzystwo imiena Fryderyka Chopina [TiFC] is the most committed promoter of the Chopin legacy. The institution's many activities include support of research and publication, maintenance of a library and museum, and organization of international conferences.

489.   Golańska, Stefania. "La Société Frédéric Chopin à Varsovie." *La musique en Pologne* 5 (1969): 11–21.

A short history of the Towarszystwo imiena Fryderyka Chopina, its early and current activities. Provides a history of the society's building, the Ostrogski Palace, and the museum collection. Also comments on Żelazowa Wola, Chopin's birthplace, and the tradition of concerts at that site.

490.   Michniewicz, Grażyna. "Geneza i działalności Instytutu Fryderyka Chopina 1934–1939" [The origins and activities of the Frederick Chopin Institute 1934–1939]. *Rocznik Chopinowski* 15 (1983): 117–141.

A history of the society, including membership, activities, and publications. Discusses the society's role in preparing the Paderewski edition of Chopin's works.

491.   Poniatowska, Irena. "Fifty Years of the Frederic Chopin Society 1934–1984." *Music in Poland* 39 (1984): 9–26.

Gives the origins of the society and its mission. Most important are the society's work in maintaining an archive, editing Chopin's music, and cataloging his works. Describes the manuscript collection and work on the Paderewski edition. Gives further information on the Chopin performance series, publication of *Annales Chopin-Rocznik Chopinowski*, and other publications related to Chopin.

492.   "Chopin Foundation of the United States." *Current Musicology* No. 24 (1977): 23–24.

Reports on the establishment of the Chopin Foundation to study the life, works, and influence of the composer. The society will conduct a piano competition every five years at the University of Miami, with the goal of sending a strong contender to the Warsaw piano competition.

493. Lissa, Zofia, ed. *The Book of the First International Musicological Congress Devoted to the Works of Frederick Chopin.* Warszawa: Polskie Wydawnictwo Muzyczne, 1963. 755 p.   ML 410.C54 I48 1960

Reviews: Maurice Brown, *Music and Letters* 45, no. 3 (1964): 268–270; Peter J. Pirie, *Music Review* 25, no. 4 (1964): 365–366; *Ruch Muzyczny* 7, no. 24 (1963): 17; Ewald Zimmermann, *Musikforschung* 19, no. 1 (1966): 96–97; *Notes* 22, no. 1 (1965): 716–717; *Musica* 19, no. 6 (1965): 327; *Beiträge zur Musikwissenschaft* 9, no. 1 (1967): 71–74.

Proceedings from a conference of February 16–22, 1960. Includes plenary papers, papers directly on Chopin and stylistic influences, and essays on Polish music history. Conference languages were Polish, English, French, German, and Russian.

494. Brennecke, Wilfred. "Internationaler musikwissenschaftlicher Chopin-Kongreß in Warschau." *Die Musikforschung* 14, no. 1 (1961): 68–72.

495. Brennecke, Wilfred. "Chopin and Polish Music: Impressions of a Visit to Warsaw." *World of Music* (February 1960): 26–29.

Reflects on the program of the international congress (see 493). Gives impressions of the popularity of sessions on Chopin's style, as well as historical problems of the influences on his style and general problems of Polish music history.

496. "Międzynarodowe Sympozjum Muzykologiczne: Chopin i Romantyzm" [International musicological symposium: Chopin and romanticism. Chopin Society, 1988]. Towarzystwo imienia Fryderyka Chopina, 1988. *Rocznik Chopinowski* 20 (1988).

Papers and discussion on performance of Chopin's music, recordings, concert repertoire, and the composer's music in the context of the nineteenth century.

497.   Poniatowska, Irena and Christiane Schreider. "Warschau, 9. Bis
        13. September 1989: II. Internationale Symposium zum Werk
        Frédéric Chopins." *Die Musikforschung* 43, no. 3 (1990): 259–260.

The theme of the conference was "Nocturne, Ballade, Scherzo."
The report makes a particular note of papers on genre. Other papers in-
vestigated the relationship of Chopin's music to literature, the reception
of his works, and analytical methods applied by scholars.

CHAPTER 5

The Chopin Legend

Chopin's music has influenced other composers and artists, and tributes to his creativity abound. A limited understanding of his life has caused his many biographers to speculate about his character and relationships. Since his death, Chopin and his music have served as icons of the Polish people. This composer-pianist has become a larger than life legend whose cultural significance is reflected in these citations.

498. Chechlińska, Zofia. "Chopin w kontekście polskiej kultury muzycznej XIX wieku" [Chopin in the context of Polish musical culture of the nineteenth century]. *Rocznik Chopinowski* 20 (1988): 60–67.

Considers the national character of Chopin's music and especially folk influences. Discusses approaches common with other Polish composers of the period.

499. Kotkowska-Bareja, Hanna. *Pomnik Chopina* [The Chopin monument]. Warszawa: Polskie Wydawnictwo Naukowe, 1970. 75 p. ML 410.C54 K6

Short account of the background of the Chopin monument in Łasiński Park.

500. Nikołajew, Wiktor. "Odtworzenie dagerotypu Fryderyka Chopin" [Reproduction of the daguerreotype of F. Chopin]. *Rocznik Chopinowski* 18 (1989): 169–171.

Extant portraits of Chopin include a daguerreotype from 1846 and photograph from 1849. Describes efforts to restore these historic images. Plates of the photographs are bound into the middle of the journal volume.

501.   Sielużycki, Czesław. "Prace chopinowskie rzeźbiarza Jean-Baptiste-August Clésingera" [Chopin works of the sculptor J.-B.-A. Clésinger]. *Rocznik Chopinowski* 16 (1984): 119–151.

Presents basic information about Clésinger and his art work. Discusses the two versions of Chopin's death mask, the bust of Chopin, and a cast of Chopin's hand. Photos of these items are provided. Clarifies the steps in the artistic process used to produce these Chopin memorabilia.

502.   Taraszkiewicz, Barbara. "Problemy fakturalne i pianistyczne w studiach Chopinowskich Leopolda Godowskiego" [Compositional and pianistic problems in the Chopin studies of L. Godowski]. *Rocznik Chopinowski* 8 (1969): 86–107.

Discusses transcriptions and arrangements of Chopin's music by Leopold Godowsky (1870–1938). Focuses on the set of études, *Studia nad etiudami Chopina*. Compares Godowsky's work to the original in order to study variations and embellishments.

503.   Swartz, Anne. "Chopin as Modernist in Nineteenth-Century Russia." *Chopin Studies 2*, pp. 35–49.

Studies the impact Chopin had on Slavophiles in nineteenth-century Russia. Reviews aesthetic judgements prevalent during the reign of Czar Nicolas I, piano manufacturing in Russia, censorship, and criticism. Considers the reception of Chopin's music, emphasizing the Western and national issues. The place of Chopin as a modernist was replaced by Tchaikovsky after 1870.

THE COMPOSER IN OTHER ARTS

Several articles have been published connecting Chopin and his work with major literary figures of nineteenth-century Poland.

504.   German, Franciszek. "Chopin i Mickiewicz" [Chopin and Mickiewicz]. *Rocznik Chopinowski* 1 (1956): 227–253.

Considers the parallel careers of Chopin and Mickiewicz (1798–1855), as well as contacts between the two artists. Chopin was familiar with Mickiewicz's works and they socialized in the same cultural circles. After presenting a chronology of their relationship, the article covers connections between Mickiewicz's poems and music.

505. German, Franciszek. "Chopin i Witwicki" [Chopin and Witwicki]. *Annales Chopin* 5 (1960): 200–224.

Gives details on the relations between Chopin and Stefan Witwicki (1801–1847), whose poems serve as the texts for a number of the composer's songs.

506. German, Franciszek. "Fryderyk Chopin i Zygmunt Krasiński" [F. Chopin and Z. Krasiński]. *Rocznik Chopinowski* 16 (1984): 105–118.

Gives details on relations between Chopin and Krasiński (1812–1859). German summary.

507. German, Franciszek. "Fryderyk Chopin i Juliusz Słowacki" [F. Chopin and J. Słowacki]. *Rocznik Chopinowski* 18 (1989): 169–171.

Provides information on Słowacki's background and contact with Chopin's music. Słowacki (1809–1849) met Chopin in Paris in 1832. Discusses general connections to the composer's music.

508. Henderson, Robert L. "Chopin and the Expressionists." *Music and Letters* 41, no. 1 (January 1960): 38–45.

Concerns the writings of Stanisław Przybyszewski (1868–1927), particularly "Chopin and Nietzsche" (1890). Reviews Przybyszewski's article, which recognizes despair in the character of Chopin. Another writing, "In Honor of a Master" (1899), presents Chopin as a true expression of the Polish people. The "immediate, spontaneous expression of sensations without reference to any formal disciplines" found in Chopin's music connects him to the expressionist movement in art and literature.

509. Opalski, Józef. *Chopin i Szymanowski w lituraturze dwudziew-stolecia międzywojennego* [Chopin and Szymanowski in literature written between World War I and II]. Kraków: Polskie Wydawnictwo Muzyczne, 1980. 224 p. ISBN 8322401035 ML 390.O68

Includes a chapter on the reception history of literature on Chopin. Addresses the Chopin legend. Reviews literature for a perspective on the reception of writing about Chopin. Considers both music writing and references in poetry and literature. Includes a bibliography and index.

510.   Stróżewski, Władysław. "Chopin i Norwid." *Rocznik Chopinowski* 19 (1987): 49–60.

511.   Stróżewski, Władysław. "Chopin and Norwid." *Chopin Studies* 3 (1990): 53–64.

Chopin is connected to Norwid (1821–1883) by philosophy; they are both romantic, but not messianistic. Discovers links between the artists, particularly references to Chopin in poems such as "Fortepian Szopena." Probes the musical associations with poetry, especially the concepts of cycle, path, universe, essentiality, and individuality. Compares *Vade-mecum* to the Preludes, op. 28.

The Chopin legend has become the subject matter for works in other art forms.

512.   Thornber, Leon. *Bitter Glory: A Novel of the Life of Chopin*. New York: Green Circle Books, 1939.   ML 3925.C55 T49

A fictionally augmented story of Chopin and George Sand. The novel begins with their meeting, introduced to each other by Liszt and Marie d'Agoult. Included are the trip to Majorca, interference of Solange in their relationship, and her wedding to Clésinger. The writing of *Lucrezia Floriani* and the manipulation of Solange "poisoned his love" for Sand. Delfina Potocka enters at the end of the novel. Sand is rejected from reconcilation at Chopin's death bed by his friends.

513.   Wilczkowska, Magdalena. "F. Chopin w plastyce polskiej na przełomie XIX i XX w." [Frederic Chopin in Polish fine arts at the turn of the nineteenth to twentieth centuries]. *Rocznik Chopinowski* 13 (1981): 97–130.

Offers an overview of artistic works related to Chopin. Relates these examples to trends in art history. Provides a catalog of 97 art works. A number of the examples are pictured in plates. Concludes with a substantial bibliography on the topic.

RECORDINGS

Several publications list sound recordings of Chopin works from their earliest production. Through these references, the performances of the most prominent Chopin interpreters can be accessed. Chopin performances through the period of long-playing records are well documented.

514. Panigel, Armand. *L'oeuvre de Frédéric Chopin: Discographie générale*. Paris: Éditions de la Revue Disques, 1949. 253 p. ML 156.5.C5 P3

Lists recordings by composition, arranged by genre presented alphabetically. Discography is international in scope, beginning with the earliest recordings. Gives a short introduction to the recording history of each piece. Includes an index of performers.

515. Kanski, Józef. *Dyskografia Chopinowska. Historyczny katalog nagrań płytowych* [A Chopin discography: A historical catalogue of recordings]. Kraków: Polskie Wydawnictwo Muzyczne, 1986. ISBN 8322403402 ML 410.C54 D6 t.3

A sequel to the Panigel discography (514) organized by piece. Gives the performer and catalog number of recordings. Includes an index of performers and photographs of prominent Chopin interpreters.

516. Kanski, Józef. "Dyskografia Chopinowska. Historyczny katalog nagrań płytowych. Mały suplement" [A Chopin discography: A historical catalog of recordings. Short supplement]. *Rocznik Chopinowski* 18 (1989): 241–243.

An addendum to 515 organized by composition.

517. Schonberg, Harold. "Frédéric Chopin: A Discography." *High Fidelity* 5, no. 4 (June 1955): 78–89.

Provides an essay on Chopin recordings plus recommended recordings of individual pieces. Reflects on Chopin performances, and addresses rubato and elements of piano technique. Refers to Long Playing recordings.

518. Zaremba, J. "Dyskografia utworów Chopina nagranych na płyty wolnoobrotowe produkcji „Polskich Nagrań" [A discography of

Chopin works recorded on LP Discs of the independent firm 'Polskie Nagrania']. *Muzyka* 4, no. 4 (1959).

Lists 137 citations. Gives the piece, performer, and catalog number. Arranged by genre.

519.   Bilica, Krzysztof. "CD-Rom z Chopinem" [A CD-ROM with Chopin]. *Ruch Muzyczny* 41, no. 2 (January 26, 1997): 21–23.

Reviews the contents of a multimedia software package compiled by Mieczysław Tomaszewski.

CHAPTER 6

Discography

The following list of notable Chopin performances on compact disc is by no means comprehensive. Organized alphabetically by artist, the compact discs selected for this Chopin discography represent both contemporary recordings and reissues of earlier performances. The intention of this addendum to previously published discographies is to provide a sample of available recordings by recognized Chopin interpreters, as referenced in *Schwann Artist Issue* (ISSN 1066–2138) and *Gramophone Classical Catalogue* (ISSN 1353–4890). In selecting recordings that best represent the Chopin performance tradition, an attempt was made to provide citations for all of Chopin's oeuvre and not merely the most popular compositions. Additional consideration was given to the various "schools" of Chopin piano performance, both inheritors of specific traditions of piano teaching and representatives of different nations.

Argerich, Martha. *Debut Recital.* Barcarolle, op. 60; Scherzos. Deutsche Grammophon 447430–2.

Argerich, Martha. London Symphony Orchestra, Claudio Abbado, cond. Concerto no. 1. Deutsche Grammophon 449719–2.

Arrau, Claudio. *Arrau, Vol. 2.* Ballades; Barcarolle, op. 60; Impromptus. Arlecchino ARL 100.

Arrau, Claudio. *Arrau, Vol. 3.* Ballades; Allegro de concert; Études; Preludes; Tarantelle. Arlecchino ARL 136.

Arrau, Claudio. *Arrau, Vol. 4.* Scherzos; Sonata, op. 58. Arlecchino ARL 160.

Arrau, Claudio. Preludes, op. 28. Odyssey YT 35934.

Arrau, Claudio. Ballade, op. 47; Études in E major, C-sharp minor, F major, F minor; Scherzo, op. 39; Waltz op. 34, no. 3. Magic Talent 48044.

Arrau, Claudio. Études, Nouvelles études. EMI Classics CDH 61016.

Ashkanazy, Vladimir. *The Young Ashkenazy, Vol. 1.* Barcarolle, op. 60; Concerto no. 2; Études op. 10 no. 1; op. 25, no. 3; Scherzos; Sonata, op. 58. Testament SBT 1045.

Ashkenazy, Vladimir. *The Young Ashkenazy, Vol. 2.* Ballade, op. 38; Mazurkas, no. 21, 29, 35, 36; Waltzes, no. 2, 6. Testament SBT 1046.

Ashkenazy, Vladimir. *Allegro de concert*; Barcarolle, op. 60; Berceuse, op. 57; Polonaises. London 452167–2.

Ashkenazy, Vladimir. Mazurkas. London 448086–2.

Ashkenazy, Vladimir. Nocturnes, op. 9, no. 2; op. 15, no. 2; op. 27, no. 1, 2; op. 32, no. 1, 2; op. 37, no. 2; Waltzes. London 430751–2.

Ashkenazy, Vladimir. Fantaisie, op. 49; Sonatas op. 35, op. 58. London 417475–2.

Ashkenazy, Vladimir. Ballades; Scherzos. London 417474–2.

Ashkenazy, Vladimir. Études. London 414127–2.

Ashkenazy, Vladimir. London Symphony Orchestra, David Zinman, cond. Concerto no. 2. London 448598–2.

Ashkenazy, Vladimir. Impromptus; Preludes, op. 28. London 417476–2.

Ax, Emmanuel. Philadelphia Orchestra, Eugene Ormandy, cond. Concertos nos. 1 and 2. RCA Victor 09026–68012–2.

Ax, Emmanuel. Mazurkas op. 6, no. 2; op. 56, no. 3; op. 59, nos. 1, 2, 3; Scherzos. CBS MK 44544.

Backhaus, Wilhelm. Berceuse, op. 57; Études; Fantaisie-impromptu, op. 66. Magic Talent 48032.

Bar-Illan, David. Ballade, op. 52. Audiofon CD 72031.

Barenboim, Daniel. Nocturnes, op. 9, no. 2; op. 15, nos. 1–3; op. 27, nos. 1, 2; op. 32, no. 1; op. 37, nos. 1, 2; op. 48, no. 1, 2; op. 55, no. 1; op. 62, no. 2; op. 72, no. 1. Deutsche Grammophon 415117–2.

Bidini, Fabio. Concerto no. 2; Impromptu, op. 36; Nocturnes; Scherzos. Polskie Nagrania PNCD 126.

Blaha, Bernadene. Ballade, op. 23; Nocturnes; Polonaise-fantaisie, op. 61; Sonata, op. 58; Grand waltzes in A-flat. Round Top RTR 8615.

Block, Michel. Mazurkas, op. 7, nos. 2, 3; op. 17, no. 4; op. 24 nos. 1, 4; op. 30, no. 4; op. 41, nos. 1, 2; op. 50, nos. 1, 2, 3; op. 56, nos. 1, 2, 3; op. 59, nos. 1, 2; op. 63, nos. 2, 3; op. 67, no. 3; op. 68, nos. 3, 4. Pro Piano PPR 224507.

Bonaventura, Anthony di. *Chopin: Late Works.* Barcarolle, op. 60; Polonaise-fantaisie, op. 61; Sonata, op. 58; Scherzos. Titanic Ti 208.

Brailowsky, Alexander. *A Retrospective, Vol. 1.* Ballade, op. 23; Études op. 10, nos. 3, 4, 5; op. 25, nos. 1, 2, 3, 9, 11, 12; Sonata, op. 35; Waltzes, op. 34, no. 1; op. 64, no. 2; op. 69, no. 1. Enterprise ENT PL 245.

Brailowsky, Alexander. Berceuse, op. 57; Ecossaises, op. 72, no. 3; Sonata, op. 58; Waltz, op. 18. APR 5501.

Brailowsky, Alexander. RCA Victor Symphony Orchestra, W. Steinberg, cond. Concertos nos. 1 and 2; Waltz in E. RCA Gold Seal 09026–61656–2.

Brendel, Alfred. Polonaise-fantaisie, op. 61; Andante spianato; Polonaises. Vanguard Classics OVC 4023.

Busoni, Ferruccio. Preludes, op. 28, nos. 1–7, 9–11, 14–16, 20, 23. Nimbus NI 8810.

Busoni, Ferruccio. Études op. 10, no. 5; op. 25, no. 5; Prelude, op. 28, no. 5; Nocturnes, op. 15, no. 2. Symposium SYM 1145.

Cliburn, Van. Sonatas, op. 35, 58. RCA Gold Seal 09026–60417–2.

Cliburn, Van. Philadelphia Orchestra, Eugene Ormandy, cond. Concerto no. 1. RCA Gold Seal 7945–2-RG.

Complete Chamber Music. Grand duo; Introduction and Polonaise, op. 3; Violoncello Sonata, op. 65; Trio, op. 8; Variations on *"La Cenerentola,"* op. posth. Canyon Classics 238.

Complete Works: Nocturnes. Henryk Stompka, op. 9, op. 27, op. 32, no. 1; Zbigniew Drzewiecki, op. 15, op. posth.; Jan Ekier, op. 32, no. 2, op. 37, op. 48, op. 55, op. 62; Lidia Grychtolówna, op. posth. Polskie Nagrania PNCD 307 A/B.

Cortot, Alfred. *Alfred Cortot: Chopin Masterworks.* Waltzes op. 18; op. 34, nos. 1–3; op. 42; op. 64, nos. 1–3; op. 69, nos. 1–2; op. 70, nos. 1–3; op. post. Sonata, op. 58. Iron Needle IN 1341.

Cortot, Alfred. *Cortot Plays Chopin: The Rare 1925–29 Recordings.* Ballades, Berceuse, op. 57; Étude, op. 25, no. 1; Impromptus; Preludes, op. 28. Music and Arts MUA 871.

Cortot, Alfred. John Barbarolli, cond. *The World of Chopin, Vol. 1.* Fantaisie, op. 49; Concerto no. 2; Sonata, op. 35. Grammofono 2000 GRM 78516.

Cortot, Alfred. Preludes, op. 28; Sonatas op. 35, op. 58. Arkadia 78510.

Cortot, Alfred. Preludes, op. 28; Ballades. Enterprise 184.

Cortot, Alfred. Ballades, Tarentelle, op. 43; Waltzes nos. 1–14. Arkadia 78509.

Cortot, Alfred. Ballades, Nocturnes, op. 9, no. 2, Sonatas op. 35, 58. Biddulph LHW 001.

Cortot, Alfred. Études; Impromptus. Arkadia 78511.

Czernicka, I. Preludes, op. 28, nos. 3, 6, 7, 8, 14, 15, 17, 19. PMG 160207.

Czerny-Stefańska, Halina. *Complete Works: Preludes.* Op. 28. Polskie Nagrania PNCD 303.

Czerny-Stefańska, Halina; Janusz Olejniczak; Tamara Granat; Waldemar Malicki; Piotr Paleczny. Warsaw Philharmonic, Kazimierz Kord, cond. Andante spianato and grande polonaise; Grande fantasia, op. 13; Introduction, Theme, and Variations, Krakowiak, op. 14; Variations on Mozart's *"La ci darem la mano."* Canyon Classics 248.

Czerny-Stefańska, Halina. Filharmonia Narodowa, Witold Rowicki, cond. *Complete Works: Concertos.* Concertos nos. 1 and 2. Polskie Nagrania PNCD 305.

Czerny-Stefańska, Halina, Warsaw Philharmonic, Witold Rowicki, cond. *Complete Works, Polonaises, Vol. 2.* Andante spianato and grande polonaise; Polonaises. Polskie Nagrania PNCD306 B.

Czerny-Stefańska, Halina; Władysław Kedra. Warsaw Philharmonic, Witold Rowicki, cond. *Complete Works: Works with Orchestra.* Andante spianato and grande polonaise; Grand fantasy; Krakowiak, op. 14; Variations op. 2. Polskie Nagrania PNCD 308.

Dang Thai Son. Preludes, op. 28, op. 45; Barcarolle. Analekta AN 27703.

Dang Thai Son. *Complete Nocturnes, Vols. 1 and 2.* Analekta AN 27701–2.

De Groote, Steven. Cape Town Symphony Orchestra, Erich Bergel, cond. Concerto no. 1. Claremont GSE 1536.

Demidenko, Nikolai. Introduction and Variations on a German Air; Scherzos; Variations, op. 2. Hyperion CDA 66514.

Demidenko, Nikolai. Allegro de concert; Polonaises; Polonaise-fantaisie. Hyperion CDA 66597.

Devos, Luc. *Nocturnes*, Vol. 2. Albumleaf in E major; Berceuse; Nocturnes; Waltzes, op. 64, nos. 1–3. Ricercar 245392.

Du Pré, Jacqueline, Daniel Barenboim, piano. Cello Sonata, op. 65. EMI Classics CDM 63184.

Ekier, Jan. *Complete Works: Ballads.* Ballads; Barcarolle, op. 60; Fantasy. Polskie Nagrania PNCD 314.

Ekier, Jan. Mazurkas. Polskie Nagrania PLN 56.

Entremont, Philip. Ballades; Scherzos; Waltzes. Odyssey MB2K 45670.

Firkusny, Rudolf. Barcarole, op. 60; Nocturnes, op. 9 no. 2, op. 27, no. 2; Polonaise op. 40, no. 2; Scherzos; Sonata, op. 58; Waltzes, op. 64, no. 2, op. 18. EMI Classics CDM 66066.

Frager, Malcolm. *Malcolm Frager Plays Chopin.* Andante spianato and grande polonaise; Sonata No. 3. Telarc CD 80280.

Friedman, Ignaz. Ballade, op. 54; Polonaise no. 9; Waltz, op. 64, no. 1. Nimbus NI 8805.

Gendron, Maurice; Keiko Toyama, piano. *Lalo and Chopin: Cello Sonatas.* Sonata, op. 65; Grand Duo; Introduction and Polonaise, op. 3. Camerata 25 CM 366.

Gieseking, Walter. *Walter Gieseking: The Homochord Recordings, 1923–25.* Études, op. 25, nos. 1, 2; Nocturnes, op. 9, no. 3, op. 15, no. 2; Polonaise, op. 53. Enterprize ENT PL 203.

Gieseking, Walter. *Gieseking: A Retrospective, Vol. 3.* Ballade, op. 47; Études, op. 25, nos. 1, 2; Nocturnes, op. 9, no. 3, op. 15, no. 2, Polonaise op. 53. Pearl PEA 9038.

Gieseking, Walter. Barcarolle, op. 60. The Classic Collector FDC 2008.

Gilels, Emil. Nocturnes, op. 55, no. 2; Ballades, Variations, op. 2. Music and Arts MUA 747.

Gilels, Emil. Philadelphia Orchestra, Eugene Ormandy, cond. Concertos no. 1 and 2. Sony Classical SBK 46336.

Gimpel, Jakob. *Jakob Gimpel: All-Chopin Recital.* Ballade, op. 23; Barcarolle, op. 60; Études op. 25, no. 1 and 11; Impromptu, op. 36; Introduction and Variations on *"Je vends des scapulaires,"* op. 12; Mazurkas, op. 30, no. 3; op. 50, no. 3; op. 56, no. 2; Nocturne, op. 62, no. 2; Scherzo, op. 20; Sonata, op. 35. Cambria CD 1070.

Godziszewski, Jerzy. *Complete Works, Vol. 3.* Preludes, op. 28. Polskie Nagrania 014.

Goode, Richard. Barcarolle, op. 60; Mazurkas, op. 7, no. 3; op. 17, nos. 1, 2, 4; op. 41, no. 3; Nocturnes; Polonaise-fantaisie, op. 61; Scherzos. Nonesuch 79452.

Gould, Glenn. Sonata, op. 58. Sony Classical SM2K 52622.

Grauwels, Marc, flute; C. Michel, harp, Variations on Rossini's *"Non più mesta."* Marco Polo 8.220441.

Grychtolowna, Lidia. *Complete Works: Scherzos and Impromptus.* Polskie Nagrania PNCD 312.

Harasiewicz, Adam. Ballade, op. 47; Mazurkas, op. 63, nos. 2, 3; Nocturnes; Polonaise op. 53; Scherzos; Sonata, op. 35. Discover International DIS 920180.

Harasiewicz, Adam. Preludes, op. 28, op. 45; Nocturnes. Philips 442266–2.

Harasiewicz, Adam. Warsaw Philharmonic Orchestra, Kazimierz Kord, cond. Concertos no. 1 and 2. Laserlight 14 003.

Hesse-Bukowska, Barbara; Ludwik Stefański; Halina Czerny-Stefańska. *Complete Works: Rondos.* Allegro de concert; Rondos. Polskie Nagrania PNCD 310.

Hofmann, Josef. *Les maîtres du piano, Vol. 1.* Polonaise, op. 53; Preludes, op. 28; Waltzes. Adès ADE 203932.

Hofmann, Josef. *The Complete Josef Hofmann, Vol. 1.* Concertos no. 1 and 2. VAI Audio VAIA/IPA 1002.

Horowitz, Vladimir. *Vladimir Horowitz: The Early Recordings, 1932–36.* Études; Impromptu, op. 29; Mazurkas, op. 7, nos. 2, 3, 7; op. 41; op. 50; Nocturnes, op. 72, no. 1; Scherzos. Enterprise ENT 188; Iron Needle IN 1303.

Horowitz, Vladimir. *The Legendary Masterworks Recordings, 1962–1973, Vol. 4.* Ballade, op. 23; Nocturnes, op. 55, no. 1; Polonaise op. 44. Sony Classical SK 53465.

Horowitz, Vladimir. Étude, op. 25, no. 7; Mazurkas, op. 33, no. 4, op. 50, no. 3; Nocturnes, op. 72, no. 1; Polonaise-fantaisie, op. 61; Polonaise, op. 44; Sonata, op. 35. CBS MK 42412.

Horowitz, Vladimir. Études, op. 10, nos. 4, 5, 8; op. 25, no. 3; Impromptu, op. 29; Mazurkas, op. 7, no. 3, op. 41, no. 2; op. 50, no. 3; Nocturne, op. 72, no. 1; Scherzo, op. 54. Magic Talent 48014..

Horszowski, Mieczysław. Nocturnes, op. 15, no. 2; op. 27, no. 2. Elektra/Nonesuch 79160–2.

Horszowski, Mieczysław. Nocturnes, op. 9, no. 2; op. 32, no. 1. Elektra/Nonesuch 79232–2.

Horszowski, Mieczysław. Vienna Symphony Orchestra. H. Swarowsky, cond. Concerto no. 1; Impromptus. Vox Box CDX2 5511.

International Chopin Piano Competition: Best Mazurka Performances, 1927–1955. Halina Czerny-Stefańska, op. 17, no. 4; op. 33, no. 3; op. 63, no. 3; op. 67, no. 4; op. 68, nos. 1, 2; Henryk Sztompka, op. 41, nos. 1, 3; op. 50, nos. 1, 2, 3; op. 67, nos. 1, 2, 3, 4; Fou Ts'ong op. 56, no. 3; op. 59, no. 1; op. 68, no. 4; Alexandre Uninsky, op. 6 no. 1; op. 63, no. 3; Jakov Zak, op. 30, no. 1; op. 63, no. 3. Polskie Nagrania PNCD 006.

International Chopin Piano Competition: Best Mazurka Performances, 1960–1985. Martha Argerich, op. 59, nos. 1, 2, 3; Marc Lafort, op. 33, nos. 1, 2, 3, 4; Garrick Ohlsson, op. 41, nos. 1, 3, 4; Ewa Poblocka, op. 59, nos. 1, 2, 3; Dang Thai Son op. 59, nos. 1, 2, 3; Irina Zaritzkaya, op. 33, nos. 1, 3; op. 50, no. 3; Krystian Zimerman, op. 24, nos. 1, 2, 4. Polskie Nagrania PNCD 007.

Katsaris, Cyprian. Andante spianato and grande polonaise, Polonaises. Sony Classical S2K 53967.

Kedra, Władysław. Warsaw Philharmonic Orchestra, Witold Rowicki, cond. *Complete Works with Orchestra.* Grand Fantasia, op. 13; Andante spianato; Krakowiak; Variations, op. 2. Polskie Nagrania PNCD 308.

Kempff, Wilhelm. Kempff Plays Chopin Vol. 1. Fantaisie-impromptu, op. 66; Impromptu, op. 29; Sonata, op. 35. London 452307–2.

Kempff, Wilhelm. *Kempff Plays Chopin, Vol. 2*. Ballades, op. 47; Fantaisie, op. 49; Polonaise-fantaisie, op. 61; Sonata, op. 58. London 452308–2.

Kilanowicz, Zofia, soprano; Katarzyna Jankowska, piano. *Songs*. Canyon Classics 237.

Kissin, Evgeni. *Chopin, Vol. 2*. Mazurkas; Sonata, op. 58. RCA Red Seal 09026-62542-2;09026–62542–4.

Kissin, Evgeni. Moscow Philharmonic Orchestra, Dmitri Kitayenko, cond. *The Legendary 1984 Moscow Concert*. Concertos nos. 1 and 2; Mazurkas, op. 63, no. 2; op. 68, no. 4; Waltz no. 14. RCA Red Seal 09026–68378.

Kissin, Evgeni. Fantaisie, op. 49; Nocturnes, nos. 12, 14; Sonata, op. 58. MK 418016.

Kissin, Evgeni. Barcarolle, op. 60; Mazurkas, op. 24, no. 4; op. 30, no. 3; op. 50, no. 3; op. 56, no. 2; op. 63, nos. 1, 2, 3; op. 68, no. 4; Scherzo, op. 31; Waltzes. MK 418017.

Kubalek, Antonin. Ballade, op. 47. Adès ADE 140762.

Kushner, Karen. *25 Mazurkas*. Opp. 6, 7, 17, 24, 30, 33. Connoisseur Society CD 4181.

Kushner, Karen. *26 Mazurkas*. Opp. 41, 50, 56, 59, 63, 67, 68. Connoisseur Society CD 4182.

Lhevinne, Rosina. National Orchestra Alumni Association, John Barnett, cond. Concerto no. 1. Vanguard VAN 60.

Lima, A. Moreira. Philharmonia Bulgarica, D. Manolov, cond. Concertos nos. 1 and 2; Krakowiak; Variations; Grande fantaisie, op. 13. Vivace G 218.

Ma, Yo-Yo. Emanuel Ax, piano, Pamela Frank, violin. Cello Sonata, op. 65.; Trio, op. 8. Sony Classical SK 53112.

Majewski, Tadeusz. Mazurkas op. 24, no. 2; op.41, no. 2; op. 7, no. 1. Emerald Classics EC 42959.

Makowska, Krystyna, Anna Wesotowska. *Introduction, Theme, and Variations—4 Hands*; Rondo. Selene CD 9404.20.

Malcuzyński, Witold. London Symphony Orchestra, Walter Susskind, cond. *Witold Malcuzynski: Artist Profile*. Concerto no. 2; Mazurkas, nos. 5, 7,15, 17, 20–23, 25, 27, 32, 41, 45, 47, 49; Sonata, op. 58; Waltzes, no. 1–14. EMI Classics ZDMB 68226.

Malikova, Anna. Turin Philharmonic Orchestra, Julian Kuvatchev, cond. Concertos nos. 1 and 2. RS Prestige 951–0019.

Michelangeli, Arturo Benedetti. *Arturo Benedetti Michelangeli: 1942–43.* Berceuse, op. 57; Mazurkas op. 33, no. 4. Teldec 93671–2.

Michelangeli, Arturo Benedetti. *The Vatican Recordings.* Andante spianato and grande polonaise. Memoria ABM 4-MEM 999001.

Michelangeli, Arturo Benedetti. Ballade op. 23, Sonatas, opp. 35, 58. Praga PR 250042.

Michelangeli, Arturo Benedetti. Berceuse, op. 57; Mazurkas op. 33, no. 4. Enterprise ENT 183.

Moravec, Ivan. *Ivan Moravec Plays Chopin, Vol. 2.* Mazurkas. VAI Audio VAIA 1092.

Moravec, Ivan. Mazurkas op. 63, no. 2; op. 68, no. 2; op. 7, no. 1; op. 30, no. 4; op. 33, no. 4; Waltzes op. 34, no. 2; op 64, no. 2, op. post.; Polonaise op. 26, no. 1; Polonaise-fantaisie, op. 61. Vox Box CDX 5103.

Moravec, Ivan. Études, op. 25, nos. 1, 7; Mazurkas op. 7, no. 5; op. 41, no. 1; op. 56, no. 2; op. 68, no. 4; Scherzos. Dorian DOR 90140.

Moravec, Ivan. Études, op. 25, no. 7; Barcarolle; Preludes, op. 28; Scherzo, op. 20. VAI Audio VAIA 1039.

Muraro, Roger. Andante spianato and grande polonaise, Polonaises, Polonaise-fantaisie. Accord ACD 205662

Nakamura, Hiroko. London Symphony Orchestra, A. Fistoulari, cond. Concerto nos. 1 and 2. Sony SMK64241.

Neuhaus, Heinrich. A. Gauk, cond. *Neuhaus Plays Chopin.* Concerto no. 1; Barcarolle, op. 60; Impromptus; Nocturnes; Polonaise-fantaisie, op. 61. Russian Disc RDCD 15007.

Novaes, Guiomar. *Guiomar Novaes Plays Chopin.* Études; Nocturnes; Sonata, op. 35. Vox Box CDX3 3501.

Novaes, Guiomar. *The Romantic Novaes.* Impromptu, op. 36; Berceuse, op. 57; Concerto, no. 1; Fantaisie-impromptu; Scherzo, op. 20; Sonata, op. 58. Vox Box CDX2 5513.

Novaes, Guiomar. Bamberg Symphony Orchestera, J. Perlea, cond. Concerto no. 1. Allegretto ACD 8006.

Ogden, John. *John Ogden: Live in Recital.* Étude op. 25, no. 1; Ballades. Altarus CD 9072.

Ogdon, John. Berceuse, op. 57; Barcarolle, op. 60; Fantaisie, op. 49; Nocturnes, op. 15, no. 1; Polonaise op. 40, no. 2; Sonata, op. 58. IMP 2008.

Ohlsson, Garrick. *Complete Works of Chopin.* Arabesque 6618, 6629, 6630, 6633, 6642, 6653, 6686, 6669.

Ohlsson, Garrick. Concerto no. 1. EMI CES5 68528–2.

Ohlsson, Garrich. 14 Nocturnes. Royal Classics ROY 6408.

Olejniczak, Janusz. Mazurkas op. 17, nos. 2, 4; op. 24, no. 4; op. 41, no. 2; Concerto no. 2. Opus 111 OPS 43–9107.

Olejniczak, Janusz. Warsaw Philharmonic Orchestra, Kazimierz Kord, cond. Grand fantasia, op. 13; Andante spianato; *Introduction, Theme and Variations*; Krakowiak; Variations on Mozart's *"La ci darem la mano."* Canyon Classics 248.

O'Rourke, Miceál. Andante spianato and grande polonaise; Ballades; Polonaise-fantaisie, op. 61. Chandos CHAN 9353.

Paderewski, Ignacy. Ballades opp. 23 and 47; Mazurkas op. 24, no. 4; Nocturnes, op. 37, no. 2; Polonaise op. 40, no. 1; Scherzos, op. 39, no. 3; Valse brilliante, op. 34, no. 1. Klavier KCD 11014.

Paderewski, Ignacy. Études, op. 10, no. 12, op. 25, nos. 1, 2, 11. Nocturnes, op. 15, no. 1; Polonaise, op. 53; Waltz, op. 64, no. 2. Enterprise ENT 182.

Perahia, Murray. Barcarolle, op. 60; Berceuse, op., 57; Fantaisie, op. 49; Impromptus. CBS MK 39708.

Perahia, Murray. Fantaisie-impromptu, op. 66; Preludes, op. 28. CBS MK 42448.

Perahia, Murray. Israel Philharmonc Orchestra, Zubin Mehta, cond. Concerto nos. 1 and 2. Sony Classical SK 44922.

Pires, Maria Joao. Royal Philharmonic Orchestra, André Previn, cond. Concerto no. 2; Preludes. Deutsche Grammophon 437817–2.

Pletnev, Mikhail. Scherzos; Barcarolle; Nocturnes; Sonata op. 35. Virgin Classics CDC 45076.

Pletnev, Mikhail. Études, op. 10, no. 5; op. 25, nos. 6, 7; Eccossaises; Fantasie, op. 49; Impromptu, op. 29; Sonata, op. 58; Waltzes op. 34, no. 1, 2. Deutsche Grammophon 453456–2.

Pogorelich, Ivo. Ballade, op. 38; Études, op. 10, nos. 8, 10; op. 25, no. 6; Mazurkas op. 59, nos. 1, 2, 3; Nocturnes, op. 55, no. 2; Polonaise op. 44; Preludes, opp. 28, 45; Scherzos, op. 39. Capriccio CDC 10024.

Pollini, Maurizio. Polonaise-fantaisie, op. 61. Exclusive EXL 22.

Pollini, Maurizio. Étude, op. 25, no. 11. Arkadia 917.

Pollini, Maurizio. Études; Polonaises; Preludes, op. 28. Deutsche Grammophon 431221–2.

Pollini, Maurizio. Ballade, op. 23; Concerto no. 1; Nocturnes, op. 15, nos. 1, 2; Polonaise, op. 53. EMI Classics CDM 66221; Angel 69004.

Pollini, Maurizio. Philharmonia Orchestra, P. Kletzki, cond. Concerto no. 1; Ballades; Nocturnes; Polonaise, no. 6. EMI Classics CDM 66221.

Pommier, Jean-Bernard. Andante spianato and grande polonaise; Polonaise-fantaisie, op. 61; Sonata, op. 58; Waltzes. Erato 92887–2.

Rachmaninoff, Serge. *The Rachmaninoff Heritage, Vol. 1.* Ballade, op. 47; Mazurkas; Nocturnes; Scherzo, op. 39; Sonata, op. 35; Waltzes. HPC 053.

Rachmaninoff, Serge. Ballade, op. 47; Nocturnes, op. 9, no. 2; Sonata, op. 35; Waltzes. RCA Gold Seal 09026–62533–2.

Reisenberg, Nadia. *Vol. 3.* Allegro de concert; Barcarole; Berceuse; Mazurkas. InSync C 4157.

Richter, Sviatoslav. London Symphony Orchestra, Kiril Kondrashin, cond. *Richter Collection, Vol. 6.* Andante spianato and grande polonaise. Historical Performers HPS 13.

Richter, Sviatoslav. *Sviatoslav Richter in Prague.* Études, op. 10, nos. 1, 2, 3, 12; op. 25, nos. 5, 6; Praga PR 254060.

Richter, Sviatoslav. *Classic Richter.* Scherzo, op. 54. Olympia OLY 580.

Richter, Sviatoslav. Ballade, op. 23; Rondos. Pyramid PYR 13507.

Richter, Sviatoslav. London Symphony Orchestra, Kiril Kondrashin, cond. Andante spianato and grande polonaise. Intaglio INCD 707–1.

Richter, Sviatoslav. Études; Nocturnes; Polonaise-fantasie, op. 61. Praga PR 254056.

Rosen, Charles. Ballade, op. 47; Barcarolle, op. 60; Polonaise-fantaisie, op. 61; Sonata, op. 35. Music and Arts MUA 609.

Rosen, Charles. New Philharmonia Orchestra, J. Pritchard, cond. Concerto no. 2. Odyssey YT 31529.

Rosen, Charles. *The Romantic Generation.* Nocturnes, op. 27, no. 2; op. 62, no. 1. Music Master 01612–67154–2.

Rostropovich, Mstislav. *Rostropovich in Recital.* Music and Arts MUA 965.

Rubinstein, Artur. London Symphony Orchestra, John Barbarolli, cond. *Artur Rubinstein Plays Chopin.* Concertos nos. 1 and 2; Nocturnes. Grammofono 2000 GRM 78554.

Rubinstein, Artur. *The Complete Mazurkas.* Enterprize ENT PL 242.

Rubinstein, Artur. Andante spianato and grande polonaise; Barcarole, op. 60; Impromptus; Nouvelles études. RCA Red Seal 5617–2-RC.

Rubinstein, Artur. Impromptus. RCA RD89911.

Rubinstein, Artur. London New Symphony Orchestra, A. Wallenstein, cond. Andante spianato and grande polonaise; Concerto No. 2; Grande fantasia, op. 13. RCA Gold Seal 60404–2-RG.

Rubinstein, Artur. Fantaisie, op. 49; Sonatas, op. 35, op. 58. RCA Red Seal 5616–2-RC.

Rubinstein, Artur. Polish National Radio Symphony Orchestra of Katowice, Jan Krenz, cond. Concertos nos. 1 and 2. Prelude PRE 2165.

Rubinstein, Artur. London New Symphony Orchestra, S. Skrowaczewski, cond. Concertos nos. 1 and 2. RCA Red Seal 5612-2-RC.

Rubinstein, Artur. Barcarolle, op. 60; Berceuse, op. 57; Preludes, op. 28; Sonata, op. 35. RCA Gold Seal 60047-2-RG; 60047-4-RG.

Schmalfuss, Peter. *The Best of Chopin.* Impromptu, op. 29; Ballade, op. 52; Études; Nocturnes; Preludes, op. 28; Sonata, op. 35; Waltzes. Eclipse 2688332 C; Point Classics 268332.

Sebok, Gyorgy. Polonaise, op. 40, no. 1; Barcarolle; Sonatas opp. 35, 58. Erato ERA SEL 98476.

Serkin, Rudolf. Études, op. 10, no. 1; op. 25, nos. 2, 11. Archipon ARC 105.

Simon, Abbey. Études; Waltzes. Vox Box CDX 5167.

Simon, Abbey. Hamburg Symphony Orchestra, H. Beissel, cond. *Complete Works for Piano and Orchestra.* Krakowiak, op. 14; Andante spianato; Concertos nos. 1 and 2; Grand Fantasy; Variations. Vox Box CDX 5002.

Slenczynska, Ruth. Études, op. 10; Ballades. ACA Digital Recording CM 20010-10.

Smendzianka, Regina. *Complete Works: Waltzes.* Polskie Nagrania PNCD 302.

Sofronitsky, Vladimir. *Russian Piano School: Vladimir Sofronitsky.* Nocturnes op. 9, no. 2; Mazurkas, op. 17, no. 3; op. 24, no. 1; op. 33, no. 3; op. 68, nos. 2, 3; op. 64, no. 1; op. 69, no. 1; op. 70, no. 3. Russian Compact Disc RCD 16288.

Sofronitsky, Vladimir. *Sofronitsky, Vol. 9.* Impromptu, op. 51; Barcarolle; Mazurkas, op. 41; op. 63; op. 33; op. 68; op. 30; op. 50; Nocturnes, op. 27; Polonaises op. 26, nos. 1, 2; Waltzes op. 69; op. 70. Arlecchino ARL 41.

Sosińska, Marta. *International Chopin Competition: Best Polonaise Performances.* Polonaise-fantaisie, op. 61; Andante spianato; Polonaises. Polskie Nagrania PNCD 014.

Sosińska, Marta. *Complete Works, Vol. 5.* Barcarolle, op. 60; Fantaisie; Sonatas, op. 35, op. 58. Polskie Nagrania PNCD 016.

Starker, János; Gyorgy Sebok, piano. Cello Sonata, op. 65. Mercury Living Presence 434358-2.

Sterczyński, Jerzy. New Polish Philharmonic Orchestra, Adam, Natanek, cond. Concerto no. 2. Selene CD 9405.21.

Sterczyński, Jerzy. Nocturne op. 9, no. 1; Mazurkas; Preludes, op. 28. Selene CD 9504.27.

Sultanow, Aleksei. Andante spianato and grande polonaise; Ballades; Polonaise, op. 53; Scherzos. Teldec 2292–46463–2 ZK.

Switala, Wojciech. Ballade op. 47; Andante spianato; Scherzos; Sonata, op. 35. Polish Radio Katowice PRK 007.

Szabó, Péter, Dénes Várjon, piano. *Chamber Music.* Grand Duo; Cello Sonata, op. 65; Trio. Hungaroton HCD 31651.

Sztompka, Henryk. *Complete Works: Mazurkas, Vols. 1 and 2.* PNCD 313A, 313B.

Tiempo, Sergio. Andante spianato and grande polonaise; Concerto no. 1. Verdi Classics VSP 6800.

Toczyńska, Stefania, mezzosoprano; Janusz Olejniczak, piano. *Songs,* op. 74, nos. 6, 9, 16, 17. Selene CD 9503.26.

Ts'ong, Fou. Polonaise-fantaisie, op. 61; Barcarolle; Berceuse; Fantaisie. Sony Classical SBK 53515.

Ts'ong, Fou. Nocturnes. Sony Classical SB2K 53249.

Watts, Andre. New York Philharmonic Orchestra, Thomas Schippers, cond. Concertos nos. 1 and 2. Sony Classical SBK 46336; SBT 46336.

Wild, Earl. Scherzos. Chesky CD44.

Wild, Earl. Études; Nouvelles études. Chesky CD77.

Wild, Earl. Royal Philharmonic Orchestra, M. Sargent, cond. Concerto no. 1. Chesky CD93.

Woytowicz, Bolesław. *Complete Works: Études.* Polskie Nagrania PNCD 304.

Woytowicz, Bolesław. *Complete Works: Preludes.* Preludes, op. 28; op. 45. Polskie Nagrania PNCD 303.

Woytowicz, Stefania, soprano; Andrzej Bachleda, tenor; Wanda Klimowicz, piano. *Complete Works: Songs.* Polskie Nagrania PNCD 315.

Yassa, Ramzi. Andante spianato and grande polonaise; Ballades. Pavane ADW 7173.

Zimerman, Krystian. Barcarolle, op. 60; Fantaisie, op. 49. Deutsche Grammophon 423090–2.

Zimerman, Krystian. Concertos nos. 1 and 2. Los Angeles Philharmonic Orchestra, C.M. Giulini, cond. Deutsche Grammophon 415 970–2GH.

Zimerman, Krystian. Berlin Philharmonic Orchestra, Herbert von Karajan, cond. Concerto no. 2. Exclusive EXL 41.

CHAPTER 7

Letters

The Chopin Letters remain the most important source of information on the composer's life and activities. The various editions of the correspondence differ in their contents, the dating of the documents, transcription from the original manuscripts, and translation. This catalog, compiled from the most significant printed collections, lists letters to and from Chopin, as well as references about him in other documents. The numbers in each reference relate to item numbers in each publication. I have presumed that the latest dating of a letter is the most accurate, but earlier considerations of date can be researched through the reference numbers. Those documents that have been included in several publications clearly relate the most insight to the composer. This catalog is intended to facilitate comparison of the interpretations.

A. *Korespondencja Fryderyka Chopina* [Correspondence of F. Chopin], 2 vols. Ed. Bronisław Edward Sydow. Warszawa: Państwowy Instytut Wydawniczy, 1955. 604 p.   ML 410.C54 A 283

B. *Correspondance de Frédéric Chopin.* Ed. Bronisław Edward Sydow. Paris: Richard-Masse, 1953–1960. 324, 416, 479 p. Paris: Revue musicale, 1981 3 vols.   ML 410.C54A283

C. *Chopin's Letters.* Ed. Henryk Opieński. Trans. E.L. Voynich. New York: Knopf, 1931. Reprint, New York: Dover, 1988. 424 p.   ISBN 0–486–25564–6 ML 410.C54A4

D. *Selected Correspondence of Fryderyk Chopin, abridged from Sydow.* Trans. and ed. Arthur Hedley. New York: McGraw-Hill, 1963. 400 p.   ML 410.C54 A2835 1979

E.   Kobylańska, Krystyna, ed. *Korespondencja Fryderyka Chopina z rodziną.* [F. Chopin's correspondence with his family]. Warszawa: Państwowy Instytut Wydawniczy, 1972. 413 p.   ML 410.C54 A238

1816   *6 December:* to Nicolas Chopin (Polish). A: 1, B: 1, C: 1, D: 1

1817   *16 June,* Warsaw: to Justyna Chopin (Polish). A: 2, B: 2, C: 2
       6 December, Warsaw: to Nicolas Chopin (Polish). A: 3, B: 3, C: 3

1818   6 December, Warsaw: to Nicolas Chopin (Polish). A: 4, B: 4, C: 4, E: 1

1823   *September,* Warsaw: to Eustachy Marylski in Pęcice (Polish). A: 5, B: 5, C: 5

1824   *10 August,* Sokołowo: to his parents in Warsaw (Polish). A: 6, B: 6, E: 2
       16 August, Szafarnia: to his family in Warsaw (Polish). A: 7, B: 7, E: 3
       19 August, Szafarnia: to Wilhelm Kolberg in Warsaw (Polish). A: 8, B: 8, C: 6
       19 August, Szafarnia: to his family in Warsaw (Polish). A: 9, B: 9, E: 4
       24 August, Szafarnia: to his family in Warsaw (Polish). A: 10, B: 10, E: 5
       27 August, Szafarnia: to his family in Warsaw (Polish). A: 11, B: 11, E: 6
       31 August, Szafarnia: to his family in Warsaw (Polish). A: 12, B: 12, E: 7
       3 September, Szafarnia: to his family in Warsaw (Polish). A: 13, E: 8
       End of summer, Sokołowo: to Jan Białobłocki in Radomin (Polish). A: 14, B: 14, C: 7

1825   *8 July,* Warsaw: to Jan Białobłocki in Sokołowo (Polish). A: 15, B: 15, C: 8
       27 November, Warsaw: to Jan Białobłocki in Sokołowo (Polish). A: 16, B: 16, C: 9
       Summer, Kowalewo: to his family in Warsaw (Polish). A: 17, B: 17, C: 10

Beginning of August, Szafarnia: to Jan Matuszyński in Warsaw (Polish). A: 18, B: 18, C: 11

28 August, to his family (Polish). A: 19, E: 9

8 September, Warsaw: to Jan Białobłocki in Sokołowo (Polish) A: 20, B: 19, C: 12

30 October, Warsaw: to Jan Białobłocki (Polish). A: 21, B: 20, C: 13, D: 4

November, Warsaw: to Jan Białobłocki (Polish). A: 22, B: 21, C: 14, D: 5

Christmas, Żelazowa Wola: to Jan Białobłocki in Sokołowo (Polish). A: 23, B: 22, C: 15

1826   *12 February*, Warsaw: to Jan Białobłocki in Bischofwerder (Polish). A: 24, B: 23, C: 16

15 May, Warsaw: to Jan Białobłocki in Sokołowo (Polish). A: 25, B: 24, C: 17, D: 6

June, Warsaw: to Jan Białobłocki in Sokołowo (Polish). A: 26, B: 25, C: 18, D: 7

18 August, Duszniki: to Wilhelm Kolberg in Warsaw (Polish). A: 27, B:26, C: 19, D: 8

19 August, Warsaw: Wojciech Żywny to F. Chopin in Duszniki (German). A: 28, B: 27

29 August, Duszniki: to Józef Elsner in Warsaw (French) A: 29, B: 28, C: 20, D: 9

2 October, Warsaw: to Jan Białobłocki in Sokołowo (Polish). A: 30, B: 29, C: 21, D: 10

1827   *8 January*, Warsaw: to Jan Białobłocki in Sokołowo (Polish). A: 31, B: 30, C: 22, D: 11

12 March, Warsaw: to Jan Białobłocki in Sokołowo (Polish). A: 32, B: 31, C: 23, D: 12

Before 8 July, Kowalewo: to his family (Polish). E: 10

Winter: to Jan Matuszyński in Warsaw (Polish). A: 33, B: 32, C: 24

1828   *9 September*, Warsaw: to Titus Wojciechowski in Poturzyń (Polish). A: 34, B: 33, C: 25, D: 13

16 September, Berlin: to his family in Warsaw (Polish). A: 35, B: 34, C: 26, D:14, E: 11

20 September, Berlin, to his family in Warsaw (Polish). A: 36, B: 35, C: 27, D: 15, E: 12

27 September, Berlin: to his family in Warsaw (Polish). A: 37, B: 36, C: 28, D: 16, E: 13

27 December, Warsaw: to Titus Wojciechowski (Polish). A: 38, B: 37, C: 29, D: 17

1829   *13 April*, Warsaw: Nicolas Chopin to Minister Stanisław Grabowski in Warsaw (Polish). A: 39, B: 38, D: 18

1 August, Vienna: to his family in Warsaw (Polish). A: 40, B: 39, C: 30, E:14

8 August, Vienna: to his family in Warsaw (Polish). A: 41, B: 40, C: 31, D: 19, E: 15

12 August, Vienna: to his family in Warsaw (Polish). A: 42, B: 41, C: 32, D: 20, E: 16

13 August, Vienna: to his family in Warsaw (Polish). A: 43, B: 42, C: 33, D: 21, E: 17

19 August, Vienna: to his family in Warsaw (Polish). A: 44, B: 43, C: 34, D: 22, E: 18

19 August, Vienna: Wilhelm Würfel to an unknown recipient in Prague (German). A: 45, B: 44

22 August, Prague: to his family in Warsaw (Polish). A: 46, B: 45, C: 35, D: 23, E: 19

26 August, Dresden: to his family in Warsaw (Polish). A: 47, B: 46, C: 36, D: 24, E: 20

12 September, Warsaw: to Titus Wojciechowski in Poturzyń (Polish). A: 48, B: 47, C: 37, D: 25

3 October, Warsaw: to Titus Wojciechowski in Poturzyń (Polish). A: 49, B: 48, C: 38, D: 26

20 October, Warsaw: to Titus Wojciechowski in Poturzyń (Polish). A: 50, B: 49, C: 39, D: 27

4 November, Antonin: Prince Anton Radziwiłł to F. Chopin in Warsaw (French). A: 51, B: 50, D: 28

14 November, Warsaw: to Titus Wojciechowski in Poturzyń (Polish). A: 52, B: 51, C: 40, D: 29

1830   *27 March*, Warsaw: to Titus Wojciechowski in Poturzyń (Polish). A: 53, B: 52, C: 41, D: 30

10 April, Warsaw: to Titus Wojciechowski in Poturzyń (Polish). A: 54, B: 53, C: 42, D: 31

17 April, Warsaw: to Titus Wojciechowski in Poturzyń (Polish). A: 55, B: 54, C: 43, D: 32

15 May, Warsaw, to Titus Wojciechowski in Poturzyń (Polish). A: 56, B: 55, C: 44, D: 33

5 June, Warsaw: to Titus Wojciechowski in Poturzyń (Polish). A: 57, B: 56, C: 45 D: 34

21 August, Warsaw: to Titus Wojciechowski in Poturzyń (Polish). A: 58, B: 57, C: 46, D: 35

31 August, Warsaw: to Titus Wojciechowski in Poturzyń (Polish). A: 59, B: 58, C: 47, D: 36

4 September, Warsaw, to Titus Wojciechowski in Poturzyń (Polish). A: 60, B: 59, C: 48, D: 37

18 September, Warsaw: to Titus Wojciechowski in Poturzyń (Polish). A: 61, B: 60, C: 49, D: 38

22 September, Warsaw: to Titus Wojciechowski in Poturzyń (Polish). A: 62, B: 61, C: 50, D: 39

5 October, Warsaw: to Titus Wojciechowski in Poturzyń (Polish). A: 63, B: 62, C: 51, D: 40

Beginning of October, Warsaw: to Clémentine Hoffman, née Tańska, in Warsaw (Polish). B: 63

12 October, Warsaw: to Titus Wojciechowski in Poturzyń (Polish). A: 64, B: 64, C: 52, D: 41

25 October: written by Konstancja Gladowska in Chopin's album (Polish). B: 65

9 November, Wrocław: to his family in Warsaw (Polish). A: 65, B: 66, C: 53, D: 42, E: 21

14 November, Dresden: to his family in Warsaw (Polish). A: 66, B: 67, C: 54, D: 43, E: 22

21 November, Prague: to his family in Warsaw (Polish). A: 67, B: 68, C: 55, D: 44, E: 23

24 November, Vienna: to Jan Matuszyński in Warsaw (Polish). A: 68, B: 69, C: 56, D: 45

1 December, Vienna: to his family in Warsaw (Polish). A: 69, B: 70, C: 57, D: 46, E:24

22 December, Vienna: to his family in Warsaw (Polish). A: 70, B: 71, C: 58, D: 47, E: 25

25 December, Vienna: to his family in Warsaw (Polish). A: 71, B: 72, C: 59, D: 48

1831 *1 January*, Vienna: to Jan Matuszyński in Warsaw (Polish). A: 73, B: 73, Hedley 49, C: 62

1 January, Vienna: to Jan Matuszyński in Warsaw (Polish). A: 74, B: 74, C: 60.

29 January, Vienna: to Józef Elsner in Warsaw (Polish). A: 75, B: 75, C: 61, D: 50

1 May, Vienna: notebook entry (Polish). A: 76, B: 76, C: 67, D: 51

2 May: Written by Joseph Slavik in Chopin's album (French). B: 77

14 May, Vienna: to his family in Warsaw (Polish). A: 77, B: 78,C: 63, D: 52, E: 26

15 May, Vienna: to Vencelas Hanka in Prague (Polish). A: 78, B: 79

28 May, Vienna: to his family in Warsaw (Polish). A: 79, B: 80, C: 64, D: 53, E: 27

June, Vienna: written by L.E. Czapek in Chopin's album (Polish). B: 81

9 June, Vienna: from Chopin's notebook (Polish). A: 76, B: 82, C: 67.

25 June, Vienna: to his family in Warsaw (Polish). A: 80, B: 83, C: 65, D: 54, E: 28

29 June, Warsaw, Nicolas Chopin to F. Chopin in Munich (French). A: 81, B: 84, D: 55, E: 29

6 July, Warsaw, Stefan Witwicki to F. Chopin in Vienna (Polish). A: 82, B: 85, D: 56

12 July, Vienna: written by Wilhelm Würfel in Chopin's album (German). B: 86

16 July, Vienna: to his family in Warsaw (Polish). A: 83, B: 87, C: 66, D: 57, E: 30

20 July, Vienna: to his family in Warsaw (Polish). B: 88, E: 31

1 September, Munich: written by an unknown author in Chopin's album (German). A: 84, B: 89

September, Stuttgart: written in Chopin's notebook (Stuttgart Journal) (Polish) A: 85, B: 90, C: 68, D: 58

18 November, Paris: to Norbert-Alfons Kumelski in Berlin (Polish). A: 86, B: 91, C: 69

1 December, Paris, Ferdinand Paër to C.P. Sotte in Paris (French). B: 92

27 November, Warsaw, Nicolas Chopin to F. Chopin in Paris (French). A: 87, B: 93, D: 60, E: 32

27 November, Warsaw: Izabela Chopin to F. Chopin in Paris (Polish). A: 88, B: 94, E: 33

27 November, Warsaw: Ludwika Chopin to F. Chopin in Paris (Polish). A: 89, B: 95, E: 34

27 November, Warsaw: Józef Elsner to F. Chopin in Paris (Polish). A: 90, B: 96, E: A2

8 December, Paris: Louis-Pierre Norblin to F. Chopin (Polish). A: 91, B: 97

12 December, Paris: to Titus Wojciechowski in Poturzyń (Polish). A: 92, B: 98, C: 70, D: 63

14 December, Paris: to Józef Elsner in Warsaw (Polish). A: 93, B: 99, C: 71, D: 64, E: A3

25 December, Paris: to Titus Wojciechowski in Poturzyń (Polish). A: 94, B: 100, C: 72, D: 65

1832 *24 February*, Warsaw: Nicolas Chopin to F. Chopin in Paris (French). A: 95, B: 101, E: 35

24 February, Warsaw: Ludwika Chopin to F. Chopin in Paris (Polish). A: 96, B: 102, E: 36

24 February, Warsaw: Justyna Chopin to F. Chopin in Paris (Polish). B: 103

13 March, Paris: to the Société des Concerts du Conservatoire in Paris (French). A: 97, B: 104, D: 67

15 April, Paris: to Józef Nowakowski in Warsaw (Polish). A: 98, B: 105, D: 69

Paris: Ferdinand Hiller in Chopin's album (German). B: 106

16 April, Paris: Felix Mendelssohn-Bartholdy in Chopin's album (French). B: 107

Spring, Paris: Antoni Orłowski to his family in Warsaw (Polish). B: 108, D: 68

28 June, Nicolas Chopin to F. Chopin in Paris (French). A: 99, B: 109, E: 37

28 June: Ludwika Chopin to F. Chopin in Paris (Polish). A: 100, B: 110

2 August, Paris: to Ferdinand Hiller in Frankfurt (French). A: 101, B: 111, C: 73, D: 71

Summer, Tours: to Auguste Franchomme in Tours (French). A: 102, B: 112

3 September, Paris: Juliusz Słowacki to his mother (Polish). A: 103, D: 72

9 September, Paris: Louis-Pierre Norblin to F. Chopin in Paris (Polish). A: 104, B: 113

10 September, Paris: to Józef Kalasant Jędrzejewicz (Polish). A: 105, B: 114, C: 75, E: 39

September, Warsaw: Nicolas Chopin to F. Chopin in Paris (French). A: 106–107, B: 115, E: 40

20 October, Paris: Anna Liszt to F. Chopin in Paris (German). A: 141, B: 116

13 November, Warsaw, Józef Elsner to F. Chopin in Paris (Polish). A: 108, B: 117, D: 73

Before 22 November, Warsaw: Józef-Kalasant Jędrzejewicz to F. Chopin (Polish). E: 41

1833 *January*, Paris: Ferdinand Hiller to F. Chopin in Paris (French). A: 109, B: 118

January, Paris: to Dominik Dziewanowski in Berlin (Polish). A: 110, B: 119, D: 74, C: 74

January, Paris: Mme. Mars to F. Chopin in Paris (French). B: 120

16 January, Paris: to the President of the Société littéraire polonaise (Polish). A: 111, B: 121, D: 75

16 January, Paris: Countess Marie d'Agoult to F. Chopin in Paris (French). A: 169, B: 122

March: Heinrich Herz to F. Chopin in Paris (French). A: 112

13 April, Warsaw: Nicolas Chopin to F. Chopin in Paris (French). A: 113, B: 123, D: 76, E: 42

13 April, Warsaw: Antoni Barciński to F. Chopin in Paris (Polish). A: 114, B: 124, E: 43

13 April, Paris: Franz Liszt to Countess Marie d'Agoult, 4 fragments (French). B: 125–128

20 June, Paris: Liszt, Chopin, and Franchomme to Ferdinand Hiller in Frankfurt-am-Main (French). A: 115, B: 129, C: 76, D: 77

20 June: Countess Marie d'Agoult to F. Chopin in Paris (French). A: 171, B: 130

20 June, Paris: Franz Liszt to Countess Marie d'Agoult in Paris (French). B: 131

20 June, Paris: Franz Liszt to Countess Marie d'Agoult in Croissy (French). B: 132

14 September, Paris: to Auguste Franchomme at Côteau (French). A: 116, B: 133, C: 77, D: 78

7 December, Warsaw: Nicolas Chopin to F. Chopin in Paris (French). A: 117, B: 134, E: 44

7 December, Warsaw: Izabela Chopin to F. Chopin in Paris (Polish). A: 118, B: 135, E: 45

7 December, Warsaw: Antoni Barciński to F. Chopin in Paris (Polish). A: 119, B: 136, E: 46

7 *December*, Warsaw: Count Michał Skarbek to F. Chopin in Paris (Polish). A: 120, B: 137, E: 47

18 December, Paris: Franz Liszt to Countess Marie d'Agoult in Paris (French). B: 138

18 December, Paris: to Julian Fontana in Paris (Polish). A: 121, B: 139

18 December, Paris: to Julian Fontana in Paris (Polish). A: 122, B: 140, C: 87

1834   *January*, Paris: François-Joseph Fétis to F. Chopin in Paris (French). A: 123, B: 141

January, Warsaw: Nicolas Chopin to F. Chopin in Paris (French). A: 126, B: 142, D: 79, E:48

13 February, Paris: Adolphe Crémieux to F. Chopin in Paris (French). A: 124, B: 143

13 February, Paris, Ernest Legouvé to F. Chopin in Paris (French).B: 144

13 February, Paris: Auguste Franchomme to F. Chopin (French). A: 144, B: 145

15 February: Adolphe Crémieux to F. Chopin (French). A: 125

26 April, Warsaw: Nicolas Chopin to F. Chopin in Paris (French). A: 127, B: 146, E: 49

26 April, Warsaw: Isabella Chopin to F. Chopin in Paris (Polish). A: 128, B: 147, D: 80, E: 50

End of May, a boat on the Rhine: to Madame Hiller in Paris (German). A: 129, B: 148, D: 82

May, Paris: Franz Liszt to Countess Marie d'Agoult in Paris (French). B: 149–51

May, Warsaw: Nicolas Chopin to F. Chopin in Paris (French). A: 130, B: 152, E: 51

May, Warsaw: Izabela Chopin to F. Chopin in Paris (Polish). A: 131, B: 153, E: 52

May, Paris: Franz Liszt to Countess d'Agoult in Paris (French). B: 154

May, Paris: Hector Berlioz to F. Chopin in Paris (French). A: 132, B: 155, D: 81

18 July, Paris: to Feliks Wodziński in Geneva (Polish). A: 133, B: 156, C: 78, D: 83

Summer, Paris: Franz Liszt to F. Chopin in Paris (French). A: 134, B: 157

25 August: Franz Liszt to Countess Marie d'Agoult in Paris (French). B: 158

7 September, Nicolas Chopin to F. Chopin in Paris (French). A: 135, B: 159, D: 85, E: 53

7 September, Warsaw: Ludwika Jędrzejewicz to F. Chopin (Polish). A: 136, B: 160, E: 54

7 September, Warsaw: Izabela Chopin to F. Chopin in Paris (Polish). A: 137, B: 161, E: 55

13 September, Paris: Franz Liszt to Countess Marie d'Agoult in Paris (French). B: 162

14 September, Warsaw: Józef Elsner to F. Chopin in Paris (Polish).A: 138, B: 163, D: 86

13 October, Paris: General Józef Dwernicki to F. Chopin in Paris (Polish). A: 140, B: 164

13 October, Paris: Antoni Orłowski to his family in Poland (Polish). B: 165, D: 87

24 November, Warsaw: Nicolas Chopin to F. Chopin in Paris (French). A: 142, B: 166, E: 56

24 November, Paris: Jan Matuszyński to his brother-in-law in Poland (Polish). B: 167, D: 84

To Julian Fontana in Paris (Polish). A: 145

1835　*23 January*, Paris: Countess Marie d'Agoult to F. Chopin in Paris (French). A: 226, B: 168

23 January, Paris: Hector Berlioz to F. Chopin in Paris (French). A: 143, B: 169

9 February, Warsaw: Nicolas Chopin to F. Chopin in Paris (French). A: 146, B: 170, E: 57

9 February, Warsaw: Ludwika Jędrzejewicz to F. Chopin in Paris (Polish). A: 147, B: 171, E: 58

9 February, Paris: to Julian Fontana in Paris (Polish). A: 148, B: 172, C: 90

27 February, Paris: General Józef Bem to F. Chopin in Paris (Polish). A: 149, B: 173

28 February, Geneva: Teresa Wodzińska to F. Chopin in Paris (Polish). A: 150, B: 174, D: 89

11 April, Warsaw: Nicolas Chopin to F. Chopin in Paris (French). A: 152, B: 175, D: 90, E: 59

12 June, Warsaw: Wojciech Żywny to F. Chopin in Paris (German). A: 153, B: 176

8 August, Vienna: Édouard Wolf to Józef Nowakowski in Warsaw (Polish). A: 154, B: 177

16 August, Karlsbad: Nicolas Chopin to Józef-Kalasant Jędrzejewicz in Warsaw (French). A: 155, B: 178, E: 60

16 August, Karlsbad, to his sisters in Warsaw (Polish). A: 156, B: 179, C: 79, D: 79, E: 61

14 September, enroute to Wrocław: Nicolas Chopin to F. Chopin (Polish and French). A: 157, B: 180, E: 62

September, Dresden: Maria Wodzińska to F. Chopin in Paris (Polish and French). A: 158, B: 181, D: 92

6 October: Felix Mendelssohn-Bartholdy to Fanny Hensel (German). A: 159, B: 182, D: 93

October, Paris: Antoine Wodziński to his mother in Dresden (Polish). A: 160, B: 183

5 December, Paris: General Józef Bem to F. Chopin in Paris (Polish). A: 161, B: 185

15 December, Warsaw: Nicolas Chopin to F. Chopin in Paris (French). A: 162, B: 186, E: 63

15 December, Warsaw: Izabela Barcińska to F. Chopin in Paris (Polish). A: 163, B: 187, E: 64

15 December, Warsaw: Ludwika Jędrzejewicz to F. Chopin in Paris (Polish). A: 164, B: 188, E: 65

15 December, Paris: to Julian Fontana in Paris (Polish). A: 165, B: 189, C: 89

28 December, Paris: Frédéric Kalkbrenner to F. Chopin in Paris (French). A: 139, B: 184, D: 88

1836   *9 January*, Warsaw: Nicolas Chopin to F. Chopin in Paris (French). A: 166, B: 190, D: 94, E: 66

9 January, Warsaw: Nicolas Chopin to Jan Matuszyński in Paris (French). A: 167, B: 191, E: A9

30 January, Paris: Marquis de Custine to F. Chopin in Paris (French). A: 168, B: 192

30 January, Paris: Charles-Valentin Alkan to F. Chopin in Paris (French). B: 193

5 February, Dresden: Teresa Wodzińska to F. Chopin in Paris (Polish). A: 170, B: 194

5 February, Paris: Marquis de Custine to F. Chopin in Paris (French). B: 195

5 February, Paris: to Camille Pleyel in Paris (French). A: 172, B: 196

14 March, Paris: to Antoni Barciński in Warsaw (Polish). A: 173, B: 197, C: 80, E: 67

18 March, Paris: Marquis de Custine to F. Chopin in Paris (French). A: 204, B: 198, D: 95

25 March, Brussels: François-Joseph Fétis to F. Chopin in Paris (French). A: 174, B: 199, D: 96

28 March, Paris: to François-Joseph Fétis in Brussels (French). A: 175, B: 200

28 March, Leipzig: Felix Mendelssohn-Bartholdy to F. Chopin in Paris (French). A: 176, B: 201, D: 97

28 March, Leipzig: Robert Schumann to F.Chopin in Paris (German). A: 177, B: 202

25–30 April, Lyon: Franz Liszt to Countess Marie d'Agoult in Geneva (French). B: 203

8 May, Warsaw: Ludwika Jędrzejewicz to F. Chopin in Paris (Polish). A: 179, B: 205, E: 69

Warsaw: Nicolas Chopin to F. Chopin in Paris (French). A: 180, B: 206, E: 70

9 May, Warsaw: Nicolas Chopin to F. Chopin in Paris (French). A: 178, B: 204, E: 68

9 May, Warsaw: Antoni Barciński to F. Chopin in Paris (Polish). A: 181, B: 207, E: 71

12 May, Paris: Anna Liszt to F. Chopin in Paris (German). A: 182, B: 208, D: 98

14 May, Paris: Fragment of letter from Franz Liszt to Countess Marie d'Agoult in Geneva (French). B: 209, D: 99

May, Paris: Fragment of letter from Franz Liszt to Countess Marie d'Agoult in Geneva (French). B: 210

May, Paris: Fragment of letter from Franz Liszt to Countess Marie d'Agoult in Geneva (French). B: 211

21 May, Paris: Fragment of letter from Franz Liszt to Countess Marie d'Agoult in Geneva (French). B: 212

30 May, Frankfurt: Ferdinand Hiller to F. Chopin in Paris (French). A: 183, B: 213, D: 100

18 June, Saint-Gratien: Marquis de Custine to F. Chopin in Paris (French). B: 214

30 June, Marquis de Custine to F. Chopin in Paris (French). A: 184, B: 215

6 July, Paris: General Józef Bem to F. Chopin in Paris (Polish). A: 185, B: 216

Beginning of July, Saint-Gratien: Marquis de Custine to F. Chopin in Paris (French). B: 217

8 September, Leipzig: Robert Schumann to F. Chopin in Dresden (German). A: 186, B: 218, D: 101

14 September, Leipzig: Robert Schumann to Heinrich Dorn in Riga (German). A: 187, B: 219, D: 102

14 September, Dresden: Teresa Wodzińska to F. Chopin in Paris (Polish). A: 188, B: 220, D: 103

15 September, Dresden: Kazimierz Wodziński to F. Chopin in Paris (Polish and French). A: 189, B: 221

15 September, Dresden: Maria Wodzińska to F. Chopin in Paris (Polish and French). A: 190, B: 222

2 October, Dresden. Teresa Wodzińska to F. Chopin in Paris (Polish). A: 191, B: 223, D: 104

2 October, Dresden: Maria Wodzińska to F. Chopin in Paris (Polish and French). A: 192, B: 224

1 November, Paris: to Teresa Wodzińska in Służewo (Polish). A: 193, B: 225, C: 81

Paris: to his family in Warsaw (Polish). B: 226

Paris: to Julian Fontana in Paris (Polish). A: 194, B: 227

13 December, Paris: to Józef Brzowski in Paris (Polish). A: 196, B: 228, D: 106

Paris: to Julian Fontana in Paris (Polish). A: 195, B: 229

Paris: to Józef Brzowski in Paris (Polish). A: 197, B: 230

Paris: Marquis de Custine to F. Chopin in Paris (French). A: 207, B: 231

Before 1837, Paris: Ernest Legouvé to F. Chopin (French). A: 199

1837 25 January, Służewo: Teresa Wodzińska to F. Chopin in Paris (Polish). A: 200, B: 232, D: 107

25 January, Służewo: Maria Wodzińska to F. Chopin in Paris (Polish and French). A: 201, B: 233

13 February, Paris: Franz Liszt to Countess Marie d'Agoult at Nohant (French). B: 234

25 February, Paris: Franz Liszt to Countess Marie d'Agoult at Nohant (French). B: 235

End of February, Warsaw: Justyna Chopin to F. Chopin in Paris (Polish). A: 202, B: 236, D: 108, E: 72

2 April, Paris: to Teresa Wodzińska in Służewo (Polish). A: 209, B: 237, C: 82, D: 111

26 March, Paris: Countess Marie d'Agoult to George Sand at Nohant (French). B: 238

28 March, Nohant: George Sand to Liszt (French). D: 110

8 April, Paris: Countess Marie d'Agoult to George Sand at Nohant (French). B: 239

14 May, Paris: to Teresa Wodzińska in Służewo (Polish). A: 211, B: 240, C: 83

mid-May, Paris: to Antoni Wodziński in Saragosse (Polish). A: 212, B: 241, C: 84, D: 113

Spring, Służewo: Marie Wodzińska to F. Chopin in Paris (French). A: 203, B: 242, D: 109

Spring, Saint-Gratien: Marquis Custine to F. Chopin in Paris (French). A: 213, B: 243, D: 114

18 June, Paris: to Teresa Wodzińska in Służewo (Polish). A: 215, B: 244, C: 85

June: George Sand to Wojciech Grzymała (French). A: 234

June: George Sand to Wojciech Grzymała (French). A: 235

5 April, Nohant: George Sand to Countess Marie d'Agoult (French). A: 210, D: 112

2 or 9 July, St. Gratien: Count Custine to F. Chopin in Paris (French). A: 216

July, London: to Julian Fontana in Paris (Polish). B: 245, D: 116

July, Paris: Julian Fontana to Stanisław Kozmian. D: 115

July, London: to an unknown correspondant in Paris (Polish). A: 117, B: 246

After 24 July, Paris: to Wojciech Grzymała in Paris (Polish). A: 218, B: 247, C: 92

14 August, Paris: to Teresa Wodzińska in Służewo (Polish). A: 219, B: 248, C: 86, D: 117

London: Felix Mendelssohn-Bartholdy to Ferdinand Hiller (German). B: 249

Służewo: Teresa Wodzińska to F. Chopin in Paris (Polish). A: 222, B: 250

Paris: Fromental Halévy to F. Chopin in Paris (French). A: 220, B: 251

Paris: to Wojciech Grzymała in Paris (Polish). A: 223, B: 252

Paris: to Wojciech Grzymała in Paris (Polish). A: 224, B: 253, C: 93

Paris: to Auguste Franchomme in Paris (French). A: 225, B: 254

Spring, Służewo: Teresa Wodzińska to F. Chopin in Paris (Polish). B: 255, D: 119

Paris: to Severin Goszczyński in Paris (Polish). B: 256
Paris: Count Custine to F. Chopin in Paris (French) A: 205
Paris: Count Custine to F. Chopin in Paris (French). A: 206

1838 *2 January*, Nohant: George Sand to Countess Marie d'Agoult in Come (French). B: 257
14 February, Paris: to Baron de Tremont in Paris (French). A: 227, B: 258
6 March: Marquis de Custine to F. Chopin (French). A: 229
Spring: Teresa Wodzińska to F. Chopin (Polish). A: 230
April or May, Paris: George Sand to Eugène Delacroix in Paris (French). A: 233, B: 259
Paris: George Sand to F. Chopin in Paris (French). A: 260, B: 260
23 May, Nohant: George Sand to Countess Carlotta Marliani in Paris (French). B: 261, D: 120
June, Paris: to Wojciech Grzymała in Paris (Polish). A: 237, B: 262, C: 91, D: 122
June, Nohant: George Sand to Wojciech Grzymała in Paris (French). B: 263, D: 121
June–July, Nohant: George Sand to Wojciech Grzymała in Paris (French). B: 264, D: 124
Paris: to Wojciech Grzymała in Paris (Polish). B: 265, D: 124
Paris: to Wojciech Grzymała in Paris (Polish). A: 236, B: 266, C: 94
10 August, Paris: to Maurice Schlesinger in Paris (French). A: 238, B: 267
Paris: Felicien Mallefille to F. Chopin in Paris (French). A: 239, B: 268
5 September, Valmont: Eugène Delacroix to Pierret in Paris (French). A: 240, B: 269
26 September, Paris: George Sand to Pierre Leroux in Paris (French). B: 270
1 or 2 November, Port-Vendres: George Sand to Countess Carlotta Marliani in Paris (French). B: 271, D: 125
8 November, Florence: Franz Liszt to Major Adolphe Pictet in Geneva (French). B: 272
9 November, Florence: Countess Marie d'Agoult to Countess Carlotta Marliani in Paris (French). A: 242, B: 273
14 November, Palma: George Sand to Countess Carlotta Marliani in Paris (French). B: 274
15 November, Palma: to Julian Fontana in Paris (Polish). A: 243, B: 275, C: 95, D: 126

November, Palma: George Sand to Mme. François Buloz in Paris (French). B: 276

21 November, Palma: to Camille Pleyel in Paris (French). A: 244, B: 277

26 November, Florence: Countess Marie d'Agoult to Major Pictet in Geneva (French). B: 278

3 December, Palma: to Wojciech Grzymała in Paris (Polish). A: 245, B: 279, C: 97, D: 127

3 December, Palma: George Sand to Wojciech Grzymała in Paris (French). B: 280

3 December, Palma: to Julian Fontana in Paris (Polish). A: 246, B: 281, C: 96, D: 128

3–14 December, Palma: to Wojciech Grzymała in Paris (Polish). A: 247, B: 282

5 December: Sainte-Beuve to Mme. Juste Olivier (French). B: 283

14 December: Palma: to Julian Fontana in Paris (Polish). A: 248, B: 284, C: 98, D: 129

14 December: Palma: George Sand to Countess Carlotta Marliani in Paris (French). B: 285

28 December: Valdemosa: to Julian Fontana in Paris (Polish). A: 249, B: 286, C: 99, D: 130

George Sand to F. Chopin (French). A: 232

1839 *10 January*, Florence: Countess Marie d'Agoult to Major Pictet in Geneva (French). B: 287

22 January, Valdemosa: to Julian Fontana in Paris (Polish). A: 250, B: 288, C: 100, D: 131

15 January, Valdemosa: George Sand to Countess Carlotta Marliani in Paris (French). B: 289

22 January, Valdemosa: to Camille Pleyel in Paris (French). A: 251, B: 290, D: 132

22 January, Valdemosa: George Sand to Countess Carlotta Marliani in Paris (French). B: 291

15 February, Barcelona: George Sand to Countess Carlotta Marliani in Paris (French). B: 292, D: 133

5 March, Marseilles: George Sand to Countess Carlotta Marliani in Paris (French) B: 293

6 March, Marseilles: George Sand to Countess Carlotta Marliani in Paris (French). B: 294

7 March, Marseilles: to Julian Fontana in Paris (Polish). A: 252, B: 295 C: 103, C: 101, D: 134

11 March, Marseilles: George Sand to Jules Boucoiran in Nimes (French). B: 296

12 March, Marseilles, to Julian Fontana in Paris (Polish). A: 255, B: 297, C: 103, D: 135

12 March, Marseilles: to Wojciech Grzymała in Paris (Polish). A: 256, B: 298, D: 136

15 March, Marseilles: George Sand to Countess Carlotta Marliani in Paris (French). B: 299

March, Marseilles: to Julian Fontana, in Paris (Polish). A: 253, B: 300, C: 102

17 March, Marseilles: to Julian Fontana in Paris (Polish). A: 257, B: 301, C: 104

17 March, Marseilles: George Sand to Countess Carlotta Marliani in Paris (French). B: 302

March, Marseilles: to Julian Fontana in Paris (Polish). A: 258, B: 303, C: 105. D: 137

20 March, Marseilles: George Sand to Countess Carlotta Marliani in Paris (French). B: 304

27 March, Marseilles: to Wojciech Grzymała in Paris (Polish). A: 259, B: 305, C: 106, D: 138

28 March, Marseille, to Ernest Canut in Palma (French). A: 260, B: 306, C: 107

12 April, Marseilles: to Wojciech Grzymała in Paris, P.S. to George Sand (Polish and French). A: 261, B: 307, C: 108, D: 139

16 April, Marseilles: to Wojciech Grzymała in Paris, P.S. to George Sand (Polish and French) A: 262, B: 308

25 April, Marseilles: to Julian Fontana in Paris (Polish). A: 263, B: 309, C: 109, D: 140

Paris: Hector Berlioz to F. Chopin in Marseilles (French). A: 264, B: 310

April, Marseilles: George Sand to Pierre Bocage in Paris (French) B: 311

27 April, Marseilles: George Sand to Hippolyte Chatiron in Nohant (French). B: 312

28 April, Marseilles: George Sand to Countess Carlotta Marliani in Paris (French). B: 313, D: 141

April, Rome: Franz Liszt to Major Pictet in Geneva (French). B: 314

4 May, Marseilles: George Sand to Countess Carlotta Marliani in Paris (French). B: 315

20 May, Marseilles: George Sand to Countess Carlotta Marliani in Paris (French). B: 316

21 May, Marseilles: to Wojciech Grzymała in Paris. P.S. to George Sand (Polish and French). A: 265, B: 317, D: 142

22 May, Naples: Sainte-Beuve to François Buloz in Paris (French).B: 318

22 May, Paris: Juliusz Słowacki to Konstantin Gaszyński in Paris (Polish). A: 266

2 June, Nohant: to Wojciech Grzymała in Paris. P.S. to George Sand. (Polish and French). A: 267, B: 319, C: 110, D: 143

9 June, Albana: Countess Marie d'Agoult to George Sand (French). B: 320

June, Nohant: to Wojciech Grzymała in Paris. P.S. by George Sand (Polish and French). A: 268, B: 321, C: 111

15 June, Nohant: George Sand to Countess Carlotta Marliani in Paris. (French). B: 322

End of June, Nohant: to Wojciech Grzymała in Paris (Polish). A: 269, B: 323, C: 113

4 July, Nohant: George Sand to Countess Carlotta Marliani in Paris (French). B: 324

8 July, Nohant: to Wojciech Grzymała in Paris. P.S. by George Sand (French). A: 270, B: 325, C: 112, D: 144

8 August, Nohant: to Julian Fontana in Paris (Polish). A: 271, B: 326, C: 114, D: 145

24 August, Nohant: George Sand to Countess Carlotta Marliani in Paris (French). B: 327

End of August, Nohant: to Julian Fontana in Paris (Polish). A: 272, B: 328

20 September, Nohant: to Wojciech Grzymała in Paris. P.S. to George Sand. (Polish and French). A: 272, B: 329, C: 115, D: 146

21 September, Nohant: to Julian Fontana in Paris (Polish). A: 274, B: 330, C: 116

25 September, Nohant: to Julian Fontana in Paris (Polish). A: 275, B: 331, C: 117, D: 147

29 September, Nohant: to Wojciech Grzymała in Paris. P.S. to George Sand. (Polish and French). A: 276, B: 332, C: 118

29 September, Nohant: to Julian Fontana in Paris (Polish). A: 277, B: 333, C: 118

1 October: to Julian Fontana in Paris (Polish). A: 278, B: 334, C: 122, D: 148

3 October, Nohant: to Julian Fontana in Paris (Polish). A: 279, B: 335, C: 120, D: 149

4 October, Nohant: George Sand to Countess Carlotta Marliani in Paris (French). B: 336

4 October, Nohant: to Julian Fontana in Paris (Polish). A: 280, B: 337, C: 121

7 October, Nohant: to Julian Fontana in Paris (Polish). A: 281, B: 338, C: 124, D: 150

8 October, Nohant: to Julian Fontana in Paris (Polish). A: 282, B: 339, C: 125, D: 151

8 October, Nohant: to Wojciech Grzymała in Paris. P.S. to George Sand (French). A: 283, B: 340, C: 123

Paris: to Charles-Valentin Alkan in Paris (French). A: 285, B: 341

15 November, Paris: to Grand-Duke de Bade in Heidelberg (French) A: 288, B: 342

15 November, Saint-Gratien: Marquis de Custine to F. Chopin in Paris (French). A: 286, B: 343

19 November, Paris: to Maurice Schlesinger in Paris (French). A: 289, B: 344

November, Paris: Marquis de Custine to F. Chopin in Paris (French). A: 287

November-December: Marquis de Custine to F. Chopin in Paris (French). A: 290

1 December, Paris: to Maurice Schlesinger in Paris (French). A: 291, B: 345

December, Vienna: Franz Liszt to Countess Marie d'Agoult in Paris (French). B: 346

14 December, Paris: to Breitkopf und Härtel in Leipzig (French). A: 292, B: 347, C: 127, D: 152

End of December, Saint-Gratien: Marquis de Custine to F. Chopin in Paris (French). A: 293, B: 348

End of December: to Julian Fontana (Polish). A: 294

1840   Paris: Marquis de Custine to F. Chopin in Paris (French). B: 349

19 January, Paris: Countess Marie d'Agoult to Franz Liszt in Vienna (French). B: 350

21 January, Paris: Countess Marie d'Agoult to Franz Liszt in Vienna (French). B: 351

25 January, Paris: Countess Marie d'Agoult to Franz Liszt in Pressburg (French). B: 352

29 January, Paris: Countess Marie d'Agoult to Franz Liszt in Pest (French). B: 353

2 February, Vienna: Franz Liszt to Countess Marie d'Agoult in Paris (French). B: 354

29 February, Paris: Marquis de Custine to F. Chopin in Paris (French). A: 151, B: 355

March, Paris: Countess Marie d'Agoult to Franz Liszt in Vienna (French). B: 356

24 March, Warsaw: Józef Elsner to F. Chopin in Paris (Polish). A: 295, B: 357

25 March, Paris: Stefan Witwicki to F. Chopin in Paris (Polish). A: 296, B: 358

3 April, Paris: Sainte-Beuve to Mr. and Mrs. Juste Olivier (French). B: 359

17 April, Paris: Stefan Witwicki to F. Chopin in Paris (Polish). B: 360

April, Paris: to Julian Fontana in Bordeaux (Polish).   B: 361

23 April, Paris: to Julian Fontana in Bordeaux (Polish). A: 298, B: 362, C: 128

Paris: to Count Louis Plater in Paris (Polish). A: 299, B: 363

3 May, Paris: to Konstantin Gaszyński in Paris (Polish). A: 300, B: 364

8 May, Paris: Countess Marie d'Agoult to Franz Liszt in London (French). B: 365

18 June, Paris: to Breitkopf und Härtel in Leipzig (French). A: 301, B: 366, C: 130, D: 153

28 June, St. Gratien: Marquis de Custine to F. Chopin in Paris (French). B: 367, D: 154

1 July, Paris: George Sand to Hippolyte Chatiron in Nohant (French). B: 368

20 July, Paris: Maurice Schlesinger to F. Chopin in Paris (French). A: 302, B: 369

30 July, Paris: to Józef Elsner in Warsaw (Polish). A: 303, B: 370, C: 131, D: 155,

Before 26 July, Paris: Hector Berlioz to F. Chopin in Paris (French). A: 304, B: 371

13 August, Cambrai: George Sand to F. Chopin in Paris (French). A: 305, B: 372, D: 155

Paris: George Sand to Marie de Rozières in Paris (French). B: 392

Paris: to Auguste Léo in Paris (French). A: 311, B: 393

Paris: to Auguste Franchomme in Paris (French). B: 394

Paris: Henri Heine to F. Chopin in Paris (French). A: 314, B: 395

18 April, Paris: George Sand to Pauline Viardot in London (French). B: 396, D: 159

20 April, London: Pauline Viardot to George Sand in Paris (French). B: 397

21 April, Paris: Countess Marie d'Agoult to Henri Lehmann (French). B: 398, D: 160

24 April: Eugène Delacroix to George Sand in Paris (French). A: 315

27 April, Paris: Marquis de Custine to F. Chopin in Paris (French). B: 399, D: 161

29 April, Paris: Stefan Witwicki to F. Chopin in Paris (Polish). A: 316, B: 400

April, Paris: to Adolphe Gutmann in Paris (French). A: 317, B: 401

4 May, Paris: to Breitkopf und Härtel in Leipzig (French). A: 318, B: 402, C: 132, D: 162

7 May, Paris: Countess Marie d'Agoult to Franz Liszt (French). B: 403, D: 163

10 May, Moscow: Alexandre-Joseph Artot to F. Chopin in Paris (French). A: 369, B: 404

18 May, Paris: Countess Marie d'Agoult to Henri Lehmann (French). B: 405, D: 164

22 May, Paris: to Antoine Schindler at Aix-la-Chapelle (French). A: 321, B: 406

June, Paris: Countess Marie d'Agoult to Franz Liszt (French). B: 407

Mid-June, Nohant: to Julian Fontana in Paris (Polish). A: 322, B: 408, C: 136, D: 166

20 June, Nohant: George Sand to Marie de Rozières in Paris (French). B: 409

20 or 27 June, Nohant: to Julian Fontana in Paris (Polish). A: 323, B: 410, C: 136, D: 166

18 July, Nohant: to Julian Fontana in Paris (Polish). A: 324, B: 411, C: 133

21 July, Nohant: to Julian Fontana in Paris (Polish). A: 325, B: 412, C: 134

26 July, Nohant: to Julian Fontana in Paris (Polish). A: 326

29 July, Paris: to Schubert et Cie. in Hamburg (French). A: 327, B: 413

29 July, Nohant: to Julian Fontana in Paris (Polish). A: 328, B: 414, C: 137

6 August, Vienna: Baron Diller de Pereira to F. Chopin in Paris (French). A: 329, B: 415

9 August, Nohant: to Julian Fontana in Paris (Polish). A: 330, B: 416, C: 138, D: 167

10 August: to Julian Fontana in Paris (Polish). A: 331, B: 417, Opieński 140

18 August, Nohant: to Julian Fontana in Paris (Polish). A: 332, B: 418, C: 141, D: 168

20 August, Nohant: to Julian Fontana in Paris (Polish). A: 333, B: 420, C: 142, D: 169

23 August, Nohant: to Pietro Mechetti. A: 334, D: 170

24 August: to Julian Fontana in Paris (Polish). A: 335, B: 419, C: 143, D: 171

29 August: George Sand to Marie de Rozières in Paris (French). B: 421

1 or 8 September, Nohant: to Julian Fontana in Paris (Polish). A: 336, B: 422, C: 144

12 September, Nohant: to Julian Fontana in Paris (Polish).A: 337, B: 423, C: 145, D: 172

13 September, Nohant: to Julian Fontana in Paris (Polish). A: 338, B: 424, C: 146, D: 173

18 September, Nohant: to Julian Fontana in Paris (Polish). A: 339, B: 425, C: 147

22 September: George Sand to Marie de Rozières in Paris (French). B: 426

25 September, Paris: to George Sand in Nohant (French). A: 340, B: 427, C: 150, D: 174

30 September, Nohant: to Julian Fontana in Paris (Polish). A: 341, B: 428, C: 151, D: 175

Marie de Rozières to Antoine Wodziński in Poland (French). B: 429

5 October, Nohant: to Maurice Schlesinger in Paris (French). A: 342, B: 430

6 October, Nohant: to Julian Fontana in Paris (Polish). A: 343, B: 431, C: 152, D: 176

6–7 October, Nohant: to Julian Fontana in Paris (Polish). A: 344,
B: 432, C: 153

9 October, Nohant: to Julian Fontana in Paris (Polish). A: 345, B:
433, C: 154, D: 177

11 October, Nohant: to Julian Fontana in Paris (Polish). A: 346

18 October, Nohant: to Julian Fontana in Paris (Polish). A: 347,
B: 434, C: 148, D: 178

20 October, Nohant: to Julian Fontana in Paris (Polish). A: 348

27 October, Nohant: to Julian Fontana in Paris (Polish). A: 349,
B: 435, C: 155, D: 180

1 November, Nohant: to Julian Fontana in Paris (Polish). A: 350,
B: 436, C: 156, D: 181

Paris: Charles-Valentin Alkan to F. Chopin in Paris (French). A:
352, B: 437

12 November, Paris: to Breitkopf und Härtel in Leipzig (French).
A: 351, B: 438, D: 182

3 December, Paris: to Breitkopf und Härtel in Leipzig (French).
A: 353, B: 439, C: 159, D: 183

4 December, Paris: George Sand to Hippolyte Chatiron in Mont-
givray (French). B: 440, D: 184

29 December, Warsaw: Ludwika Jędrzejewicz to F. Chopin in
Paris (Polish). A: 355, B: 441, E: 75

30 December, Warsaw: Nicolas Chopin to F. Chopin in Paris
(French). A: 354, B: 442, D: 185, E: 76

Paris: to Stefan Witwicki in Paris (Polish). A: 356, B: 443

1842   *18 January*, Paris: Countess Marie d'Agoult to Ferdinand Hiller
(French). B: 444

February, Paris: to Josephine Turowska in Paris (Polish). A: 357,
B: 445, C: 158

2 February, Paris: Ernest Legouvé to F. Chopin in Paris (French)
A: 358

15 February, Paris: Giocomo Meyerbeer to F. Chopin in Paris
(French). B: 446

16 February: Joseph Filtsch to his parents in Hungary. D: 186

8 March, Paris: Joseph Filtsch to his parents in Hungary. D: 187

21 March, Warsaw: Nicolas Chopin to F. Chopin in Paris
(French) A: 360, B: 447, D: 188, E: 77

21 March, Warsaw: Ludwika Jędrzejewicz to F. Chopin in Paris
(Polish). A: 361, B: 448, E: 79

21 March, Warsaw: Justyna Chopin to F. Chopin in Paris (Polish). A: 359, B: 449, E: 78

23 April, Paris: Stefan Witwicki to F. Chopin in Paris (Polish). A: 362, B: 450

Paris: to Wojciech Grzymała in Paris (Polish). A: 363, B: 451, C: 160

Paris: to Wojciech Grzymała in Paris (Polish). A: 364, B: 452

Spring, Paris: to Camille Pleyel in Paris (French). B: 453

Spring, Paris: to Charles Valentin Alkan in Paris (French). A: 366, B: 454

After 20 April, Paris: George Sand to Pauline Viardot (French). B: 455

9 May, Nohant: George Sand to Marie de Rozières (French). A: 368, D: 189

25 May, Nohant: to Wojciech Grzymała in Paris (Polish). A: 370, B: 456

30 May: Eugène Delacroix to George Sand in Nohant (French). A: 371

31 May, Nohant: to Wojciech Grzymała in Paris (Polish). A: 367, B: 459, C: 166, D: 190

2 June, Warsaw: Józef Elsner to F. Chopin in Paris (Polish). A: 372, B: 457

2 June, Warsaw: Józef Damse to F. Chopin in Paris (Polish). A: 373, B: 458

7 June, Nohant, Eugène Delacroix to Pierret (French). A: 374, B: 460

22 June, Nohant: Eugène Delacroix to Pierret (French). A: 375, B: 461, D: 191

End of June, Paris: Eugène Delacroix to George Sand in Nohant (French). A: 376

June-July: Adam Mickiewicz to F. Chopin (Polish). A: 378

Summer, Paris: to Mrs. Franchomme in Paris (French). A: 379

8 July, Paris: Eugène Delacroix to George Sand in Paris (French). A: 380

27 July, Nohant: to Wojciech Grzymała in Paris (Polish). A: 382, B: 462, C: 162

18 July, Nohant: to Camille Pleyel in Paris (French). A: 381, B: 463, C: 139

9 August, Paris: Eugène Delacroix to Gustav Planche in Naples (French). A: 383

19 August, Paris: Joseph Filtsch to his parents in Hungary. D: 192

16 October, Warsaw: Nicolas Chopin to F. Chopin in Paris (French). A: 384, B: 464, D: 193, E: 80

16 October, Warsaw: Ludwika Jędrzejewicz to F. Chopin in Paris (Polish). A: 385, B: 465, E: 81

16 or 17 October, Warsaw: Izabela Barcińska to F. Chopin in Paris (Polish). A: 386, B: 466, E: 82

17 October, Paris: Stefan Witwicki to F. Chopin in Paris (Polish). A: 387, B: 467

8 November, Paris: to Józef Elsner in Warsaw (Polish). A: 388, B: 468, C: 164

9 November, Paris: Joseph Filtsch to his parents. D: 194

12 November, Paris: George Sand to Hippolyte Chatiron at La Châtre. (French). B: 469

12 November, Paris: George Sand to Charles Duvernet: (French). B: 470, D: 195

29 November, Paris: Karl Filtsch to his parents. D: 196.

30 November, Paris: to Tomasz Nidecki in Warsaw (Polish). B: 471, A: 389, C: 165

30 November, Paris: Frédéric Kalkbrenner to F. Chopin in Paris (French). B: 472

30 November, Paris: Joseph Filtsch to his parents. D: 197

Paris: unknown addressee (French). A: 390, B: 473.

December, Paris: George Sand to Gustave Papet at Chateau d'Ars (French). B: 474

10 December, Paris: to Caroline Oury in London (French). A: 391, B: 475, C: 129, D: 198

15 December, Paris: to Breitkopf und Härtel in Leipzig (French). A: 392, B: 476, C: 167, D: 199

Paris, to Camille Pleyel in Paris (French). A: 377

Paris: to Camille Pleyel in Paris (French). A: 393, B: 477

Paris: Adam Mickiewicz to F. Chopin in Paris (Polish). B: 478

End of December, Paris: Stefan Witwicki to F. Chopin in Paris (Polish). A: 394, B: 479

30 December, Paris: Joseph Filtsch to his parents (German). D: 200

Paris: to Adolphe Cichowski in Paris (Polish). A: 395, B: 480

Ernest Legouvé to F. Chopin in Paris (French). A: 365

1843   *20 January*, Paris: Joseph Filtsch to his parents (German). D: 201

25 January, Paris: to Thomas Nidecki in Warsaw (Polish). A: 396, B: 481, C: 169

26 *February*, Poznan: Franz Liszt to F. Chopin in Paris (French). A: 397, B: 482, D: 202

26 *April*, Paris: Joseph Filtsch to his parents (German). D: 203

Paris: to Doctor Molin in Paris (French). A: 398, B: 483

11 *May*, Paris: George Sand to Hippolyte Chatiron (French). B: 484

22 *May*, Nohant: George Sand to Pauline Viardot (French). B: 485

6 *June*, Nohant: George Sand to Maurice Dudevant in Paris (French). B: 486, D: 204

16 *June*, Nohant: to Sophie Rozengart in Paris (French). A: 400, B: 487

Chaillot: Solange Dudevant to Maurice Dudevant in Nohant (French). A: 399, B: 488

Summer, Nohant: George Sand to Pierre Bocage in Paris (French). B: 489, D: 205

22 *July*, Nohant: to Maurice Schlesinger in Paris (French). A: 401, B: 490, C: 171

Summer, Nohant, to Wojciech Grzymała in Paris (Polish). A: 402, B: 491, C: 172

12 *August*, Nohant: George Sand to Countess Carlotta Marliani (French). B: 492, D: 206

14 *August*, Paris: to George Sand at Nohant (French). A: 403, B: 493, C: 173, D: 207

8 *September*, Paris: Eugène Delacroix to George Sand in Nohant (French). A: 404

2 *October*, Nohant: to Auguste Léo in Paris (French). A: 405, B: 494, D: 208

2 *October*, Nohant: George Sand to Countess Carlotta Marliani in Paris (French). B: 495

End of October, Nohant: to Wojciech Grzymała in Paris (Polish). A: 406, B: 496, C: 168, D: 209

Nohant: George Sand to Countess Carlotta Marliani (French). B: 497

15 *October*: to August Léo in Paris (French). A: 407, B: 498

Fall, Nohant: Solange Dudevant to Maurice Dudevant in Paris (French). A: 413

End of October, Nohant: George Sand to Countess Carlotta Marliani in Paris (French). B: 499, D: 210

Early November, Nohant: George Sand to Marie de Rozières in Paris (French). B: 500, D: 211

3 November, Paris: to George Sand in Nohant (French). A: 409,
    B: 501, C: 174, D: 212

Nohant: George Sand to Countess Carlotta Marliani in Paris
    (French). B: 502

Nohant: Solange Dudevant to Maurice Dudevant in Paris (French).
    A: 503, B: 503

13 November, Paris: Adolphe Cremieux to F. Chopin in Paris
    (French). A: 408, B: 504

17 November, Nohant: George Sand to Maurice Dudevant in
    Paris (French). B: 505

26 November, Nohant: George Sand to Maurice Deduvant in
    Paris (French). B: 506, D: 213

26 November, Paris: to George Sand in Nohant (French). A: 412,
    B: 507, C: 195, D: 214

Autumn, Paris: Clementine Hoffmann-Tańska to F. Chopin in
    Paris (Polish). A: 410, B: 508

Paris: to an unknown addressee in Paris (Polish). A: 411, B: 509

10 December, Paris: to Breitkopf und Härtel in Leipzig (French).
    A: 414, B: 510, C: 176

19 December, Paris: to Härtel in Leipzig (French). A: 415, B:
    511, C: 170, D: 215

Paris: to Stefan Witwicki in Paris (Polish). A: 416, B: 512

Paris: to an unknown addressee in Paris (Polish). A: 417, B: 513

Winter, Paris: to Sophie Rozengart in Paris (Polish). A: 418, B: 514

Winter, Paris: to Sophie Rozengart in Paris (Polish). A: 419

Winter, Paris: George Sand to Doctor Molin in Paris (French). A:
    420, B: 515

1844   *13 January*, Paris: Sainte-Beuve to F. Chopin in Paris (French).
    B: 516

Paris: Ernest Legouvé to F. Chopin in Paris (French). A: 198, B:
    517

12 May, Paris: George Sand to Doctor Molin in Paris (French).
    A: 422

26 May, Paris: George Sand to Auguste Franchomme in Paris
    (French). A: 421, B: 518

29 May, Paris: George Sand to Justyna Chopin in Warsaw (French).
    A: 432, B: 519, D: 217, E: A12

13 June, Warsaw: Justyna Chopin to George Sand in Paris
    (French). A: 424, B: 520, D: 218, E: A13

June, Warsaw: Antoni Barciński to F. Chopin in Paris (Polish). A: 425, B: 521, E: 83

June, Warsaw: Izabela Barcińska to F. Chopin in Paris (Polish). A: 426, B: 522, E: 84

June, Nohant: George Sand to F. Chopin in Nohant (French). A: 427, B: 523

16 July, Paris: to Breitkopf und Härtel in Leipzig (French). A: 428, B: 524, C: 177

July, Nohant: to Marie de Rozières in Paris (French). A: 429, B: 525, D: 220

26 July, Nohant: to Wojciech Grzymała in Paris (Polish). A: 430, B: 526, C: 178, D: 221

Nohant: George Sand to Wojciech Grzymała in Paris (French). B: 527

1 August, Nohant: to Auguste Franchomme in Paris (French). A: 432, B: 528, C: 179

2 August: August Franchomme to F. Chopin in Nohant (French). A: 433

2 August, Nohant: to August Franchomme in Paris (French). A: 434, B: 529, C: 180

5 August, Nohant: to August Franchomme in Paris (French). A: 435, B: 530, C: 181

Summer, Nohant: George Sand to Ludwika Jędrzejewicz in Warsaw (French). A: 431, B: 531, D: 219, E: A14

11 August, Nohant: to Marie de Rozières in Paris (French). A: 436, B: 532, D: 222

26 August, Dresden: Karol Lipiński to F. Chopin in Paris (Polish). A: 437, B: 533

End of August, Paris: to Wojciech Grzymała in Paris (Polish). A: 438, B: 534, C: 182, D: 223, E: A15

End of August, Nohant: George Sand to Ludwika Jędrzejewicz in Paris (French). A: 439, B: 535

3 September, Orleans: to Marie de Rozières in Paris (French). A: 440, B: 536, C: 185

7 September, Nohant: to Marie de Rozières in Paris (French). A: 441, B: 537, C: 186

11 September, Nohant: to Marie de Rozières in Paris (French). A: 442, B: 538, C: 187

18 September, Nohant: to Ludwika Jędrzejewicz in Warsaw (Polish). A: 443, B: 539, C: 188, D: 224, E: 85

18 September, Nohant: George Sand to Ludwika Jędrzejewicz in Warsaw (French). A: 444, B: 540, E: A16

20 September, Nohant: to Auguste Franchomme in Paris (French). A: 445, B: 541, C: 189, D: 225

23 September, Paris: to George Sand at Nohant (French). A: 446, B: 542, C: 190, D: 226

23 October, Nohant: to Marie de Rozières in Paris (French). A: 447, B: 543, C: 191

31 October, Nohant: to Marie de Rozières in Paris (French). A: 448, B: 544, C: 192, D: 227

31 October, Nohant: to Ludwika Jędrzejewicz in Warsaw (Polish). A: 449, B: 545, C: 192, D: 227, E: 86

3 November, Berlin: Felix Mendelssohn-Bartholdy to F. Chopin in Paris (French). A: 450, B: 546, D: 229

13 November, Nohant: to Marie de Rozières in Paris (French). A: 451, B: 547, C: 194, D: 230

21 November, Nohant: to Marie de Rozières in Paris (French). A: 452, B: 548, C: 195

21 November, Nohant: George Sand to Countess Carlotta Marliani in Paris (French) B: 549

28 November, Nohant: George Sand to Marie de Rozières in Paris (French). B: 550

2 December, Paris: to George Sand in Nohant (French). A: 453, B: 551, C: 196, D: 231

5 December, Paris: to George Sand at Nohant (French). A: 454, B: 552, C: 197, D: 232

Paris: to Adolphe Cichowski in Paris (Polish). A: 455, B: 553

Paris: to Adolphe Cichowski in Paris (Polish). B: 554

Paris: to Adolphe Cichowski in Paris (Polish). B: 555

Paris, to Adolphe Cichowski in Paris (Polish). B: 556

18 December, Fontainebleu: Bodhan Zaleski to F. Chopin in Paris (Polish). A: 457, B: 557

Paris: to Marie de Rozières in Paris (French). A: 459, B: 558, C: 183

Paris: Wojciech Grzymała to F. Chopin in Paris (Polish). A: 461, B: 559

Paris: to Wojciech Grzymała in Paris (Polish). B: 560

Paris, to Adolphe Cichowski in Paris (Polish). A: 463, B: 561

Paris: to Adolphe Cichowski in Paris (Polish). B: 562

December, Paris: to Maurice Schlesinger in Paris (French). A: 467, B: 563, D: 233

Paris: Clementine Hoffman-Tańska to F. Chopin in Paris (Polish). A: 469, B: 564

Paris: Eugène Delacroix to F. Chopin in Paris (French). A: 470

Paris: Eugène Delacroix to F. Chopin in Paris (French). A: 471, B: 565

Paris: Ernest Legouvé to F. Chopin in Paris (French). A: 458, B: 566

To Adolphe Cichowski in Paris (Polish). A: 456

Paris: to Wojciech Grzymała in Paris (Polish). A: 460

To Adolphe Cichowski in Paris (Polish). A: 464, 465, 466

1845   Paris: to August Franchomme in Paris (French). A: 468, B: 567

31 January, Paris: Frédéric Kalkbrenner to F. Chopin in Paris (French). A: 473, B: 568

Paris: to Adolphe Cichowski in Paris (Polish). A: 476, B: 569

February: Juliusz Słowacki to his mother (Polish). A: 475

Paris: to Adolphe Cichowski in Paris (Polish). A: 477, B: 570

After 5 March, Paris: to Sophie Rozengart in Paris (Polish). A: 479, B: 571

Paris: Ernest Legouvé to F. Chopin in Paris (French). B: 572

22 March, Paris: George Sand to Stefan Witwicki (French). A: 480

23 March, Paris: to Stefan Witwicki (Polish). A: 481, B: 573, C: 198, D: 234

March, Paris: Eugène Delacroix to F. Chopin in Paris (French). A: 478, B: 574

Paris: to Adolphe Cichowski in Paris (Polish). A: 482, B: 575

Paris: to Adolphe Cichowski in Paris (Polish). A: 483, B: 576

Paris: to Adolphe Cichowski in Paris (Polish). A: 484, B: 577

Paris: George Sand to Ludwika Jędrzejewicz in Warsaw (French). A: 486, B: 578, D: 244

10 April, Paris: to an unknown addressee (French). A: 485, B: 579

Paris: Eugène Delacroix to F. Chopin in Paris (French). B: 580, D: 235

Paris: to Antoni Kątski in Paris (Polish). A: 487, B: 581

Paris: to Krystian Ostrowski in Paris (Polish). A: 472, B: 582

8 July, Nohant: to Auguste Léo in Paris (French). A: 488, B: 583, D: 236

8 July, Nohant: to Wojciech Grzymała in Paris (Polish). A: 489, B: 584, C: 201

Summer, Nohant: George Sand to Ludwika Jędrzejewicz in Warsaw (French). A: 490, B: 585

Nohant: George Sand to Ludwika Jędrzejewicz in Warsaw (French). A: 491, B: 586

18 July, Nohant: to his family in Warsaw (Polish). A: 492, B: 587, C: 202, D: 237, E: 87

21 July, Nohant: to Marie de Rozières in Paris (French). A: 493, B: 588, C: 203

1 August, Nohant: to Józef-Kalasant and Ludwika Jędrzejewicz in Warsaw (French). A: 494, B: 589, C: 205, D: 238, E: 88

29 November, Nohant: George Sand to F. Chopin in Paris (French). A: 241, B: 590, D: 240

Autumn, Nohant: to Marie de Rozières in Paris (French). A: 495, B: 591, C: 184

8 October, Paris: to Felix Mendelssohn-Bartholdy in Berlin (French). A: 496, B: 592, D: 239

9 October, Nohant: to Auguste Léo in Paris (French). A: 497, B: 593

Autumn, Nohant: George Sand to Ludwika Jędrzejewicz in Warsaw (French). A: 498, B: 594

9 November, Nohant: to Auguste Franchomme in Paris (French). B: 595

6 or 7 December: to Wojciech Grzymała in Paris (Polish). A: 499, B: 596

7 December, Paris: to Marie de Rozières in Paris (French). A: 500, B: 597

Paris: Ernest Legouvé to F. Chopin in Paris (French). B: 598

End of December, Paris: to Adolphe Cichowski in Paris (Polish). A: 501, B: 599

12–26 December, Paris: to his family in Warsaw (Polish). A: 504, B: 600, C: 206, D: 241, E: 89

25 December, Paris: Frédéric Kalkbrenner to F. Chopin in Paris (French). A: 502, B: 601, D: 242

Paris: to Wojciech Grzymała in Paris (Polish). A: 503, B: 602, C: 218

Paris: to Doctor Molin in Paris (French). A: 506, B: 603

Paris: to Doctor Molin in Paris (French). A: 507, B: 604

End of December, Warsaw: Justyna Chopin to F. Chopin in Paris (Polish). A: 505, B: 605, D: 243, E: 90

1846 *March*, Paris: George Sand to Ludwika Jędrzejewicz in Warsaw (French). A: 510

Spring, Paris: George Sand to Ludwika Jędrzejewicz in Warsaw (French). B: 606, D: 245

1 May, Paris: George Sand to Maurice Dudevant in Guillery (French). A: 512, B: 607, D: 246

Late Spring, Nohant: George Sand to Ludwika Jędrzejewicz in Warsaw (French). B: 608

Franz Liszt to F. Chopin in Paris (French). A: 513, B: 609

9 May, Nohant: George Sand to Countess Carlotta Marliani in Paris (French). B: 610

Pentecost, Nohant: to Marie de Rozières in Paris (French). A: 514, B: 611, C: 207, D: 247

3 June, Nohant: George Sand to Maurice Dudevant (French). B: 612

20 June, Nohant: George Sand to Countess Carlotta Marliani in Orbec (French). B: 613

8 July, Nohant: to August Franchomme in Paris (French). A: 515, B: 614, D: 249

10 August, Paris: Eugène Delacroix to George Sand in Nohant (French). A: 516

19 August, Nohant: Eugène Delacroix to Fr. Villot (French). A: 517, B: 615

August, Nohant: to Wojciech Grzymała in Paris (Polish). A: 518, B: 616

30 August, Nohant: to Auguste Franchomme in Paris (French). A: 519, B: 617, C: 204, D: 250

30 August, Nohant: to Auguste Léo in Paris (French). A: 520, B: 618

End of summer, Nohant: George Sand to Ludwika Jędrzejewicz in Warsaw (French). A: 521, B: 619

1 September, Nohant: to Marie de Rozières in Paris (French). A: 522, B: 620, C: 208

9 September, Nohant: to Auguste Léo in Paris (French). A: 523, B: 621

12 September: Eugène Delacroix to George Sand (French). D: 251

13 September, Nohant: to Auguste Franchomme in Paris (French). A: 525, B: 622

20 September, Nohant: George Sand to Countess Carlotta Marliani (French). B: 623

22 September, Nohant: to Auguste Franchomme in Paris (French).
A: 526, B: 624

22 September, Nohant: to Mme Robio in Milan (French). A: 527,
B: 625

24 September, Nohant: George Sand to Charles Poncey (French).
D: 252

11 October, Nohant: to his family in Warsaw (Polish). A: 528, B:
626, C: 209, D: 253, E: 91

October, Nohant: George Sand to Ludwika Jędrzejewicz in Warsaw (French). A: 529, B: 627, E: A17

9 November, Nohant: F. Chopin to August Franchomme in Paris
(French). A: 530

19 November, Paris: to Breitkopf und Härtel in Leipzig (French).
A: 531, B: 628, C: 210

25 November, Paris: to George Sand in Nohant (French). A: 532,
B: 629, C: 211, D: 254

8 December, Paris: Prince and Princess Adam Czartoryski to F.
Chopin in Paris (Polish). A: 533, B: 630

12 December, Paris: to George Sand in Nohant (French). A: 535,
B: 631, C: 212, D: 255

15 December, Paris: to George Sand in Nohant (French). A: 536,
B: 632, C: 212, D: 256

Paris: to an unknown addressee in Paris (Polish). A: 537, B: 633,
C: 217

Miss Mars to F. Chopin. A: 538

25 December: Félicité de Lamennais to Jane Stirling. A: 539

29 December, Paris: Eugène Delacroix to F. Chopin in Paris
(French). A: 540, B: 634

End of December, Paris: to Wojciech Grzymała in Paris (Polish).
A: 542, B: 635, C: 214

30 December, Paris: to George Sand in Nohant (French). A: 541,
B: 636, C: 221, D: 257

End of December, Paris: to Brandus in Paris (French). A: 543, B:
637

End of December, Paris: Lamennais to F. Chopin (French). A:
534, B: 638

Edmund Chojecki to F. Chopin in Paris. A: 546

Aleksander Jełowicki to F. Chopin. A: 547

1847   *12 January*, Paris: to George Sand in Nohant (French). A: 548, B:
639, C: 222, D: 258

17 January, Paris: to George Sand in Nohant (French). A: 549, B: 640, C: 223, D: 259

Paris: Ernest Legouvé to F. Chopin in Paris (French). A: 550

Before 20 January, Paris: Ernest Legouvé to F. Chopin in Paris (French). A: 551

20 January: Ernest Legouvé to F. Chopin (French). A: 552

Ernest Legouvé to F. Chopin (French). A: 553

4 February, Paris: to Wojciech Grzymała in Paris (Polish). A: 545, B: 641, C: 220

Paris: to Wojciech Grzymała in Paris (Polish). A: 555

4 February, Paris: to Wojciech Grzymała in Paris (Polish). A: 556, B: 643, C: 216, D: 260

10 February: Franz Liszt to Countess Marie d'Agoult in Paris (French). B: 642

Paris: to Wojciech Grzymała in Paris (Polish). A: 557

Paris: to Wojciech Grzymała in Paris (Polish). B: 644

10 February, Paris: to Józef Nowakowski in Paris (Polish). A: 558, B: 646, C: 224, D: 261

17 February, Paris: to Wojciech Grzymała (Polish). A: 554, B: 645, C: 225, D: 262

Paris: Bodhan Zaleski to F. Chopin in Paris (Polish). A: 508, B: 647

Paris: to Wojciech Grzymała in Paris (Polish). A: 544, B: 648, C: 219

28 March, Paris: to his family in Warsaw (Polish). A: 560, B: 650, C: 227, D: 263, E: 92

10 April, Paris: to George Sand in Nohant (French). A: 259, B: 649, C: 226, D: 264

21 April, Paris: to George Sand in Nohant (French). A: 561, B: 651, C: 228, D: 265

29 April, Paris: to George Sand in Nohant (French). A: 262, B: 652, C: 229, D: 266

8 May, Nohant: Jean-Baptiste-Auguste Clésinger to Maurice Dudevant in Guillery (French). B: 653

8 May, Nohant: George Sand to Marie de Rozière in Paris (French). D: 267

12 May, Warsaw: Emile Jenike to F. Chopin in Paris. P.s. of Józef Elsner (Polish). A: 564, B: 654

12 May, Nohant: George Sand to Wojciech Grzymała in Paris (French). B: 655, D: 269

12 May, Paris: Eugène Delacroix to George Sand (French). D: 268

12 May, Nohant: George Sand to Adolf Gutmann (French). D: 270

15 May, Paris: to George Sand in Nohant (French). A: 269, B: 656, C: 230, D: 271

Before 20 May, Nohant: George Sand to Marie de Rozières in Paris (French). A: 568

May, Paris: to Solange Dudevant in Nohant (French). A: 571, B: 657

June, Nohant: George Sand to Wojciech Grzymała in Paris (French). A: 572

8 June, Paris to his family in Warsaw (Polish). A: 573, B: 658, D: 273, E: 93

June, Nohant: George Sand to Ludwika Jędrzejewicz in Warsaw (French). A: 574, B: 659, E: A18

30 June, Paris: to Breitkopf und Härtel in Leipzig (French). A: 575, B: 660, D: 274

July, Nohant: George Sand to Marie de Rozières in Paris (French). B: 661

18 July, La Châtre: Solange Clésinger to F. Chopin in Paris (French). A: 576, B: 662, D: 275

21 July, Paris: to Solange Clésinger in La Châtre (French). A: 577, B: 663, C: 233, D: 276

24 July, Paris: to George Sand in Nohant (French). A: 579, B: 664, D: 277

28 July, Nohant: George Sand to F. Chopin in Paris (French). B: 665, D: 278

17 September, Paris: to Wojciech Grzymała in Paris (Polish). A: 580, B: 666, C: 234

18 September, Paris: to Solange Clésinger in Besançon (French). A: 581, B: 667, C: 235, D: 279

21 September, Paris: Baron Billing de Carbine to F. Chopin in Paris (French). A: 582, B: 668, D: 280

30 September, Besançon: Solange Clésinger to F. Chopin (French). A: 583, B: 669, D: 281

1 October, Paris: to Auguste Franchomme in Paris (French). A: 584, B: 670

2 October, Paris: to Solange Clésinger in Besançon (French). A: 585, B: 671, D: 282, C: 236,

Paris: to Solange Clésinger (French). A: 591, B: 672, C: 237

16 October, Paris: to Auguste Léo in Paris (French). A: 586, B: 673

9 November, La Châtre: Solange Clésinger to F. Chopin in Paris (French). A: 587, B: 674, D: 283

19 November, Dresden: Pauline Viardot to George Sand in Nohant (French). B: 675, D: 284

19 November, Dresden: Louise Viardot to George Sand in Nohant (French). B: 676

20 November, Paris: Eugène Delacroix to George Sand in Nohant (French). A: 588

24 November, Paris: to Solange Clésinger in Guillery (French). A: 589, B: 677, C: 238, D: 285

14 December, Paris: to Solange Clésinger in Guillery (French). A: 590, B: 678, D: 286

17 December, Paris: to Hippolyte Blotnicki in Paris (Polish). A: 592, B: 679

Winter, Paris: to Auguste Franchomme in Paris (French). A: 593, B: 680

Paris: to Auguste Franchomme in Paris (French). A: 594, B: 681

25 December–6 January, 1848, Paris: to his family in Warsaw (Polish). A: 597, B: 682, C: 239, D: 287, E: 94

Paris: Eugène Delacroix to F. Chopin in Paris (French). A: 284, B: 683

Paris: Princess Czartoryska to F. Chopin in Paris (French and Polish). A: 596, B: 684

31 December, Paris: to Solange Clésinger in Guillery (French). A: 595, B: 685, C: 240, D: 288

1848 *January*, Paris: to Louis-Pierre Norblin in Paris (Polish). A: 598, B: 686

7 February, Nohant: George Sand to Maurice Dudevant in Paris (French). B: 687, D: 289

10 February, Paris: to Ludwika Jędrzejewicz in Warsaw (Polish). A: 600, B: 688, C: 241, D: 290, E: 95

February, Paris: Marquis de Custine to F. Chopin in Paris (French). A: 228, B: 689

11 February, Paris: to his family in Warsaw (Polish). A: 601, B: 690, C: 242, D: 291, E: 96

12 February, Nohant: George Sand to Maurice Dudevant in Paris (French). B: 691, D: 292

15 February, Paris: Jacob Meyerbeer to F. Chopin in Paris (French). A: 602

Before 16 February, Paris: F. Chopin to Mrs. Dorval in Paris (French). A: 603

16 February, Nohant: George Sand to Maurice Dudevant in Paris (French). B: 692, D: 293

February, Paris: Marquis de Custine to F. Chopin in Paris (French). B: 693, D: 295

17 February, Paris: Jean-Baptiste-Auguste Clésinger to F. Chopin in Paris (French). A: 605, B: 694

17 February, Paris: to Solange Clésinger in Guillery (French). A: 604, B: 695, C: 243, D: 294

18 February: Jean-Baptiste-Auguste Clésinger to F. Chopin in Paris (French). A: 599, B: 696

February, Warsaw: Justyna Chopin to F. Chopin in Paris (Polish). A: 606, B: 697, E: 97

Paris: to Adolphe Cichowski in Paris (Polish). A: 607, B: 698

Paris: to Adolphe Cichowski in Paris (Polish). A: 608, B: 699

3 March, Paris: to Solange Clésinger in Guillery (French). A: 609, B: 700, C: 244, D: 296

5 March, Warsaw: Justyna Chopin to F. Chopin in Paris (Polish). A: 611, B: 701, D: 298, E: 98

5 March, Paris: to Solange Clésinger in Guillery (French). A: 610, B: 702, C: 245, D: 297

Paris: Edmond Combes to George Sand in Paris (French). B: 703

Paris: to Wojciech Grzymała in Paris (Polish). B: 704, C: 249

8 March, Guillery: Solange Clésinger to F. Chopin in Paris (French). A: 612, B: 705

11 March, Paris: to Solange Clésinger in Guillery (French). A: 613, B: 706, C: 246, D: 299

22 March, Paris: to Solange Clésinger in Guillery (French). A: 614, B: 707, C: 247

Around 25 March, Guillery: Solange Clésinger to F. Chopin in Paris (French). A: 615, B: 708

4 April, Paris: to Julian Fontana in New York (Polish). A: 616, B: 709, C: 248, D: 300

April, Paris: Karol Gavard to Mr. Hall in London. A: 617

18 April, Paris: to Doctor Mollin in Paris (French). A: 618, B: 710, D: 301

19 April, Paris: George Sand to Maurice Dudevant in Nohant (French). B: 711

21 April, London: to Wojciech Grzymała in Paris (Polish). A: 619, B: 712, C: 250, D: 302

24 April, London: to Charles-François Szulczewski (Polish). A: 620, B: 713

1 May, London: to Auguste Franchomme in Paris (French). A: 621, B: 714, C: 251, D: 303

3 May, Leipzig: Ignace Moscheles to F. Chopin in London (French). A: 622, B: 715

4 May, London: to Wojciech Grzymała in Paris (Polish). A: 624, B: 717, C: 252, D: 304

6 May, London: to Adolphe Gutmann in Paris (French). A: 623, B: 716, C: 252, D: 305

13 May, London: to Wojciech Grzymała in Paris (Polish). A: 625, B: 718, C: 254, D: 306

21 May, Nohant: George Sand to Jules Boucoiran (French). B: 719

1 June, London: to Marie de Rozières in Paris (French). B: 720, D: 307

2 June, London: to Wojciech Grzymała in Paris (Polish). A: 627, B: 721, C: 255, D: 308

10 June: George Sand to Pauline Viardot in London (French). B: 722

30 June, London: to Solange Clésinger in Paris (French). A: 628, B: 723

30 June, London: to Marie de Rozières (French). D: 309

July, London: Jane Welsh Carlyle to Jane Stirling in London (English). A: 629, B: 724, D: 310

6 July, London: to Ignace Krzyżanowski in London (Polish). A: 630, B: 725, C: 256, E: 99

8 July, Paris: Marie de Rozières to Ludwika Jędrzejewicz in Warsaw (French). B: 726

8–17 July, London: to Wojciech Grzymała in Paris (Polish). A: 631, B: 727, C: 257, D: 311

End of July, London: to Wojciech Grzymała in Paris (Polish). A: 632, B: 728, C: 258, D: 312

1 August, London: to Camille Pleyel in Paris (French). A: 633, B: 729

6 August-Edinburgh–11 August-Calder House: to Auguste Franchomme in Paris (French). A: 634, B: 730, C: 259, D: 313

15 August, Calder House: to Camille Pleyel in Paris (French). A: 635, B: 731, D: 314

18 August, Calder House: to Julian Fontana in London (Polish). A: 636, B: 732, C: 260, D: 315

10–19 August, Calder House: to his family in Warsaw (Polish). A: 638, B: 733, C: 261, D: 316, E: 100

19 August, Calder House: to Wojciech Grzymała in Paris (Polish). A: 637, B: 734, C: 262

4 September, Johnston-Castle: to Wojciech Grzymała in Paris (Polish). A: 639, B: 735, C: 263, D: 317

11 September, Johnston-Castle: Camille Pleyel in Paris (French). A: 640, B: 736

1 October, Keir: to Wojciech Grzymała in Paris (Polish). A: 641, B: 737, C: 264, D: 318

2 October, Keir: to Marie de Rozières in Paris (French). A: 642, B: 738, C: 268, D: 319

3 October, Edinburgh: to Wojciech Grzymała in Paris (Polish). A: 643, B: 739, C: 265, D: 320

16 October, Calder House: to Adolphe Gutmann in Heidelberg (French). A: 644, B: 740, C: 266

21 October, Hamilton Palace: to Wojciech Grzymała in Paris (Polish). A: 645, B: 741, C: 269, D: 321

30 October, Edinburgh: to Wojciech Grzymała in Paris (Polish). A: 646, B: 742, C: 270–71, D: 322

3 November, London: to Adam Lyszczyński in Edinburgh (Polish). A: 647, B: 743, C: 272

17 and 18 November, London: to Wojciech Grzymała in Paris (Polish). A: 648, B: 744, C: 267, D: 323

20 November, London: to Marie de Rozières in Paris (French). A: 649, B: 745, C: 273, D: 324

London: to Dr. Mallan in London (French). A: 650, B: 746

21 November, London: to Wojciech Grzymała in Paris (Polish). A: 651, B: 747, C: 275, D: 325

London: to Dr. Mallan in London (French). A: 652, B: 748

22 November, London: to Solange Clésinger in Paris (French). A: 653, B: 749, C: 274, D: 326

23 November, London: Princess Marcelline Czartoryska to Władysław Czartoryski in Paris (Polish). A: 654, B: 750

13 December, Dusseldorf: Ferdinand Hiller to F. Chopin in Paris (French). A: 655, B: 751

1849 *19 or 26 January*, Paris: to Napoleon Orda in Paris (Polish). B: 752, C: 291

30 January, Paris: to Solange Clésinger in Guillery (French). A: 656, B: 753, C: 276, D: 327

15 February, Paris: Pauline Viardot to George Sand in Nohant (French). A: 657, B: 754, D: 328

5 April, Paris: to Solange Clésinger in Guillery (French). A: 658, B: 755, C: 277, D: 329

13 April, Paris: to Solange Clésinger in Guillery (French). A: 659, B: 756, C: 278, D: 330

14 May, Guillery: Solange Clésinger to F. Chopin in Paris (French). A: 660, B: 757

F. Chopin to Wojciech Grzymała in Paris (Polish). A: 661

16 May, Würzburg: Princess Marcellina Czartoryska to Władysław Czartoryski in Paris (Polish). A: 662, B: 758, D: 331

Paris: to Wojciech Grzymała in Paris (Polish). B: 759

19 May, Chaillot: to Solange Clésinger in Guillery (French). A: 664, B: 760, C: 279

Chaillot: to Adolphe Cichowski in Paris (Polish). A: 663, B: 761

Chaillot: to Adolphe Cichowski in Paris (Polish). A: 665, B: 762

9 June, Champrosay: Eugène Delacroix to Mme. de Forget in Paris (French). A: 666, B: 763

18 June, Chaillot: to Wojciech Grzymała in Paris (Polish). A: 668, B: 764, C: 280, D: 333

22 June, Chaillot: to Wojciech Grzymała in Paris (Polish). A: 669, B: 765, C: 281

25 June, Chaillot: to Ludwika Jędrzejewicz in Warsaw (Polish). A: 670, B: 766, C: 282, D: 334, E: 101

June, Warsaw: Justyna Chopin to F. Chopin (Polish). A: 667, D: 332, E: 102

Chaillot: to Adolphe Cichowski in Paris (Polish). A: 671, B: 767

2 July, Chaillot: to Wojciech Grzymała (Polish). A: 672, B: 768, C: 283

4 July, Chaillot: to Solange Clésinger in Guillery (French). A: 673, B: 769, C: 284, D: 335

10 July, Chaillot: to Wojciech Grzymała in Paris (Polish). A: 673, B: 770, C: 284, D: 335

16 July, Aix-la-Chapelle: Countess Delfina Potocka to F. Chopin (Polish). A: 676, B: 771, D: 337

July, Paris, Mme Grille de Beuzelin to George Sand (French). A: 675, B: 772, D: 338

19 July, Nohant: George Sand to Mme Grille de Beuzelin in Paris (French). A: 677, B: 773, D: 339

28 July, Chaillot: to Wojciech Grzymała in Paris (Polish). A: 678, B: 774, C: 286, D: 340

Chaillot: to Napoleon Orda in Paris (Polish). A: 679, B: 775, C: 291

3 August, Chaillot: to Wojciech Grzymała in Paris (Polish). A: 680, B: 776, C: 287, D: 341

August, Chaillot: to Auguste Franchomme in Paris (French). A: 683, B: 777, C: 289

14 August, Chaillot: to Marie de Rozières in Chaudfontaine, P.S. from Ludwika Jędrzejewicz (French). A: 681, B: 778, C: 288, D: 342,

Chaillot: to Adolphe Cichowski in Paris (Polish). A: 682, B: 779

20 August, Paris: to Titus Wojciechowski in Karlsbad (Polish). A: 684, B: 780, C: 290, D: 343

1 September, Nohant: George Sand to Mme Grille de Beuzelin in Paris (French). A: 686, B: 781, D: 344

1 September, Nohant: George Sand to Ludwika Jędrzejewicz in Paris (French). A: 685, B: 782

12 September, Paris: to Titus Wojciechowski in Ostende (Polish). A: 687, B: 783, C: 252, D: 345

17 September, Paris: to Auguste Franchomme in Tours (French). A: 688, B: 784, C: 293, D: 346

17 October, Paris: Ludwika Jędrzejewicz to Józef-Kalasant Jędrzejewicz in Warsaw. P.S. from Princess Marcelline Czartoryska (Polish). A: 689, B: 785, D: 347

Between the death and funeral of Chopin, Paris: Wojciech Grzymała to Auguste Léo (French). A: 695, B: 786, D: 348

21 October, Paris: Abbé Alexandre Jelowicki to Mme. Xavier Grocholska in Warsaw (Polish). A: 692, B: 787

Paris: Pauline Viardot to George Sand in Nohant (French). A: 696, B: 788

22 October, Paris: Adolphe Gutmann to Melle. Heinefetter in Mannheim (German). A: 693, B: 789

29 October, Paris: Eugène Delacroix to an unknown adressee in Paris (French). A: 694, B: 790

2 November, Paris: Eugène Delacroix to Ludwika Jędrzejewicz in Paris (French). A: 697, B: 791

8 November, Champrosay: Eugène Delacroix to an unknown addåressee (French). A: 699, B: 792

8 November, Paris: Wojciech Grzymała to Auguste Léo (French). A: 698, B: 793

Chopin's last written words. A: 689, C: 294

Author Index

Work Index

Subject Index

About the Author

William Smialek is Vice President for Academic Affairs and Dean of the Faculty at Midway College in Midway, Kentucky. He formerly served as Professor of Music and Dean of Academic Affairs at Jarvis Christian College in Hawkins, Texas. He completed the Ph.D. in musicology at the University of North Texas. During the 1979–80 academic year, he studied in Poland as a Fulbright Scholar. His publications include *Polish Music: A Research and Information Guide* and *Ignacy Feliks Dobrzyński and Musical Life in Nineteenth-Century Poland.*

Composer Resource Manuals
Guy A. Marco, *General Editor*